Life in Society 3

LISTENING

SPEAKING

Academic Encounters
2nd Edition

Kim Sanabria
Series Editor: Bernard Seal

CAMBRIDGE
UNIVERSITY PRESS

CAMBRIDGE
UNIVERSITY PRESS

32 Avenue of the Americas, New York, NY 10013-2473, USA

Cambridge University Press is part of the University of Cambridge.

It furthers the University's mission by disseminating knowledge in the pursuit of education, learning and research at the highest international levels of excellence.

www.cambridge.org
Information on this title: www.cambridge.org/9781107673144

First published 2004
Second edition 2012
8th printing 2015

Printed in Hong Kong, China, by Golden Cup Printing Company Limited

A catalog record for this publication is available from the British Library.

Library of Congress Cataloging in Publication Data

Sanabria, Kim, 1955-
[Academic listening encounters]
Academic encounters, life in society, level 3 : listening and speaking / Kim Sanabria. -- 2nd ed.
p. cm. -- (Academic encounters. Life in society)
"Audio production: John Marshall Media. Video production: Steadman Productions"--T.p. verso.
Previous ed.: 2004.
Includes index.
ISBN 978-1-107-67314-4 (Student's book with DVD)
1. English language--Textbooks for foreign speakers. 2. Listening--Problems, exercises, etc.
3. Social problems--Problems, exercises, etc. 4. Readers--Social problems.
5. English language--Sound recordings for foreign speakers. I. Title.

PE1128.S218 2012
428.2'4--dc23

2012012503

ISBN 978-1-107-67314-4 Student's Book with DVD
ISBN 978-1-107-69784-3 Class Audio CDs
ISBN 978-1-107-62547-1 Teacher's Manual

Additional resources for this publication at www.cambridge.org/academicencounters

Art direction, book design, and photo research: Integra
Layout services: Integra
Audio production: John Marshall Media
Video production: Steadman Productions

Table of Contents

Scope and sequence

Unit 1: Belonging to a Group • 1

	Content	Ⓛ Listening Skills	Ⓢ Speaking Skills
Chapter 1 Marriage, Family, and the Home page 3	**Interview 1** Growing up in a Large Family **Interview 2** Family Stories **Lecture** Family Lessons	Listening for factual information Listening for details Listening for stressed words	Sharing your opinion Responding to questions with short answers Thinking critically about the topic Asking and answering questions
Chapter 2 The Power of the Group page 22	**Interview 1** Living with Teenagers **Interview 2** Expressions About Groups **Lecture** Culture Shock: Group Pressure In Action	Listening for specific information Listening for main ideas Listening for tone of voice	Sharing your opinion Personalizing the topic Thinking critically about the topic Conducting a survey Studying a syllabus

Unit 2: Gender in Society • 43

	Content	Ⓛ Listening Skills	Ⓢ Speaking Skills
Chapter 3 Gender Roles page 45	**Interview 1** Bringing up Children **Interview 2** Growing up as a Boy or Girl **Lecture** The Benefits of Single Gender Education for Girls	Listening for specific information Listening for opinions Drawing inferences	Personalizing the topic Answering multiple-choice questions Sharing your opinion Conducting and discussing a class experiment Sharing your point of view Thinking critically about the topic
Chapter 4 Gender Issues Today page 64	**Interview 1** Gender Discrimination in the Workplace **Interview 2** Gender Inequality at Home and in the Workplace **Lecture** Gender and Language	Listening for specific information Listening for tone of voice	Examining graphics Answering multiple-choice questions Answering true/false questions Thinking critically about the topic Conducting an interview and discussing your findings Applying what you have learned

V Vocabulary Skills	**N** Note Taking Skills	Learning Outcomes
Reading and thinking about the topic Examining vocabulary in context Guessing vocabulary from context	Personalizing the topic Main ideas and supporting details Organizing your notes in columns	Prepare and deliver an oral presentation on an aspect of group dynamics
Reading and thinking about the topic Examining vocabulary in context Building background knowledge on the topic Guessing vocabulary from context	Organizational phrases Organizing your notes in outline form Copying a lecturer's diagrams and charts	

V Vocabulary Skills	**N** Note Taking Skills	Learning Outcomes
Reading and thinking about the topic Personalizing the topic Building background knowledge on the topic Examining vocabulary in context Guessing vocabulary from context	Using symbols and abbreviations Using your notes to make an outline	Prepare and deliver an oral presentation to demonstrate and support a particular point of view on a topic
Reading and thinking about the topic Building background knowledge on the topic Examining vocabulary in context Guessing vocabulary from context	Using telegraphic language	

V Vocabulary Skills	N Note Taking Skills	Learning Outcomes
Reading and thinking about the topic Examining vocabulary in context Building background knowledge on the topic Guessing vocabulary from context	Summarizing what you have heard Choosing a format for organizing your notes	Prepare and deliver an oral presentation as a group on an aspect of media and society
Reading and thinking about the topic Building background knowledge on the topic Examining vocabulary in context Guessing vocabulary from context	Recording numerical information Organizing your notes as a map	

V Vocabulary Skills	N Note Taking Skills	Learning Outcomes
Reading and thinking about the topic Building background knowledge: Technical terms Examining vocabulary in context Organizing vocabulary: Technical terms Guessing vocabulary from context	Clarifying your notes Using your notes to answer test questions Applying what you have learned	Prepare and deliver an oral presentation on a topic related to crime
Reading and thinking about the topic Examining vocabulary in context Guessing vocabulary from context	Recording numerical information Using your notes to ask questions and make comments Summarizing what you have heard	

Academic Encounters: Preparing Students for Academic Coursework

The Series

Academic Encounters is a sustained content-based series for English language learners preparing to study college-level subject matter in English. The goal of the series is to expose students to the types of texts and tasks that they will encounter in their academic course work and provide them with the skills to be successful when that encounter occurs.

Academic Content

At each level in the series, there are two thematically paired books. One is an academic reading and writing skills book, in which students encounter readings that are based on authentic academic texts. In this book, students are given the skills to understand texts and respond to them in writing. The reading and writing book is paired with an academic listening and speaking skills book, in which students encounter discussion and lecture material specially prepared by experts in their field. In this book, students learn how to take notes from a lecture, participate in discussions, and prepare short presentations.

Flexibility

The books at each level may be used as stand-alone reading and writing books or listening and speaking books. They may also be used together to create a complete four-skills course. This is made possible because the content of each book at each level is very closely related. Each unit and chapter, for example, has the same title and deals with similar content, so that teachers can easily focus on different skills, but the same content, as they toggle from one book to the other. Additionally, if the books are taught together, when students are presented with the culminating unit writing or speaking assignment, they will have a rich and varied supply of reading and lecture material to draw on.

A Sustained Content Approach

A sustained content approach teaches language through the study of subject matter from one or two related academic content areas. This approach simulates the experience of university courses and better prepares students for academic study.

Students benefit from a sustained content approach

Real-world academic language and skills

Students learn how to understand and use academic language because they are studying actual academic content.

An authentic, intensive experience

By immersing students in the language of a single academic discipline, sustained content helps prepare them for the rigor of later coursework.

Natural recycling of language

Because a sustained content course focuses on a particular academic discipline, concepts and language recur. As students progress through the course, their ability to work with authentic language improves dramatically.

Knowledge of common academic content

When students work with content from the most popular university courses, they gain real knowledge of these academic disciplines. This helps them to be more successful when they move on to later coursework.

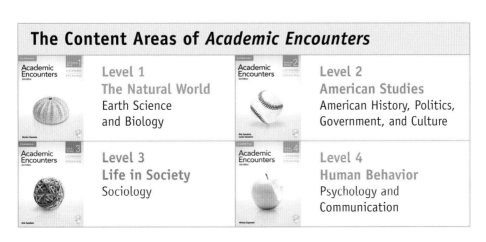

The Content Areas of *Academic Encounters*

Level 1
The Natural World
Earth Science and Biology

Level 2
American Studies
American History, Politics, Government, and Culture

Level 3
Life in Society
Sociology

Level 4
Human Behavior
Psychology and Communication

Academic Skills

Academic Encounters, Listening and Speaking
teaches skills in 4 main areas. A set of icons
highlights which skills are practiced in each exercise.

Listening Skills

The listening skills tasks are designed
to help students develop strategies
before listening, while listening, and
after listening.

Speaking Skills

Students learn how to participate
in formal and informal situations at
universities, including sharing opinions,
presenting research, and creating
extended oral presentations. These skills
and tasks were carefully selected to
prepare students for university study.

Vocabulary Skills

Vocabulary learning is an essential part of
academic preparation. Tasks throughout
the books focus on particular sets of
vocabulary that are important for reading
in a particular subject area as well as
vocabulary from the Academic Word List.

Note Taking Skills

In order to succeed in university courses,
students need to be able to take notes
effectively. Each unit teaches a range
of note taking skills, ranging from
organizational strategies and listening
for key numbers to using your notes to
prepare for tests.

Preparing for Authentic Listening

B Answer the questions according to the information in the passage.

1. What are two different approaches to controlling crime?
2. How could educational and social programs help lower the crime rate?

C Read these questions and share your answers with a partner.

1. Which of the two different approaches to controlling crime do you think is more effective? Why?
2. Do you think your community has a high crime rate or a low crime rate? Explain.

2 Examining graphics ⑤

A Look at the illustration below. It shows how often, on average, crimes are committed in the United States. Fill in the blank with the crime you think is represented by each clock. Then compare your answers with a partner.

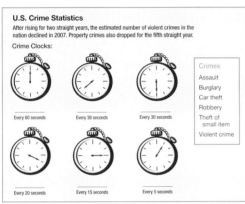

U.S. Crime Statistics

After rising for two straight years, the estimated number of violent crimes in the nation declined in 2007. Property crimes also dropped for the fifth straight year.

Crime Clocks:

Every 60 seconds	Every 38 seconds	Every 30 seconds
Every 20 seconds	Every 15 seconds	Every 5 seconds

Crimes
Assault
Burglary
Car theft
Robbery
Theft of small item
Violent crime

Source: U.S. Department of Justice/Federal Bureau of Investigation

B Check your answers at the bottom of the page. Did any of the information surprise you?

Answers:
Violent crime: Every 20 seconds
Robbery: every 60 seconds
Assault: Every 15 seconds
Burglary: Every 38 seconds
Car theft: Every 30 seconds
Theft of small item: every 5 seconds

> Students develop a range of **skills** to help them **anticipate and prepare** for the listening tasks.

INTERVIEW 1 Preventing Juvenile Crime

1 Examining vocabulary in context ⓥ

Here are some words and phrases from the interview with David, printed in **bold** and given in the context in which you will hear them. They are followed by definitions.

I think the media **exacerbates** the problem: *makes worse*

We have thousands of security guards in the schools and **metal detectors**, too: *machines that can detect guns, knives, and other weapons made of metal . . .* and the kids get **searched** as they go into school: *physically examined*

Put them on a **one-to-one basis**, and they're usually very friendly: *with one other person*

The problem is that social support systems have really
fallen apart: *become ineffective*

Kids should be doing . . . a **structured** program of activities: *organized*

The **funding** for programs like those has been cut: *money*

But we also need **harsher** punishments: *stronger, more serious*

Drug crimes carry a maximum **sentence** of 20 years or life imprisonment: *punishment*

2 Listening for main ideas ⓛ ⓝ ⑤

A Read these questions before you listen to the interview with David.

1. What does David think causes young people to commit crimes?

2. Does David believe that schools are usually bright, welcoming places?

3. How do kids feel about school?

4. Does David believe that some kids are violent by nature?

5. What kinds of programs does David think schools should organize?

6. Does David believe in harsh punishments?

> The first listenings are **authentic interviews**, in which students develop **skills such as listening for main ideas and details.**

Academic Listening and Speaking

3 Listening for tone of voice 🅛 🅢

🔊 **A** Listen to excerpts from the interviews. Circle one item that best completes the statements.

Excerpt 1
Kelly is discussing differences between now and the past. When she speaks about the future of the post office, she sounds
   a. sure of her opinion.
   b. amused.
   c. confident.

Excerpt 2
Nina is talking about how she surfs the Internet. When she explains how long she can spend online, she sounds
   a. serious.
   b. proud.
   c. as if she has mixed feelings.

Excerpt 3
Richard is talking about his feelings toward the media. He says he has to make a confession. He sounds
   a. apologetic.
   b. tired.
   c. confused.

Excerpt 4
Orlando is discussing the digital divide in his country. He sounds
   a. as if the situation is confusing.
   b. worried.
   c. optimistic.

B Compare your answers with a partner. Explain why you chose those answers.

> **Post-listening activities** help students **analyze and understand** the authentic inverviews.

AFTER THE INTERVIEWS

1 Sharing your opinion 🅢
A Read the statements below. For each statement, check (✓) whether you agree strongly, agree, are not sure, disagree, or disagree strongly.

	Agree strongly	Agree	Not sure	Disagree	Disagree strongly
1. We are brainwashed by the news we see on TV.					
2. Being online for many hours makes people antisocial.					

Chapter 6 *Impact of the Media on Our Lives*

> Students then study and practice using discrete **speaking skills**, as they express their own opinions about the **academic content**.

3 In Your Own Voice

In this section, you will conduct some research on the way society expects men and women to behave. You will observe groups of men and women and discuss what you see with other students. You will also practice using language to describe an experiment.

Conducting and discussing a class experiment 🅢 🅝

> Academic lecturers and textbooks often refer to research conducted by experts. It is interesting to try to copy the experts' research experiments on a smaller scale. Doing your own experiments will give you an idea of some of the steps involved in doing more extensive research. It can also provide interesting information and lead to unexpected findings.

A Read some background information.

Many researchers have conducted experiments on gender. Some experiments have involved observing the speech and behavior of thousands of men and women. These experiments have concluded that most men and women obey the "rules" and act the way that society expects them to act.

For example, Robin Tolmach Lakoff discovered that women and men speak in different ways. Women tend to be very polite and apologize more frequently than men do. Deborah Tannen also found that there are differences between the way men and women communicate. For example, men often exchange information, but women tend to discuss their emotions. Because of these differences, men and women often misunderstand each other. Joyce McCarl Nielsen et al., discovered that men and women not only speak differently but also behave differently, acting in ways that seem common for their gender. They made a list of the ways men and women behave in public and discovered that people usually adopt accepted behavior.

B Prepare your own experiment. Look at the list of behaviors below. With a partner, decide if each behavior is commonly associated with men or women, and write *M* (male) or *F* (female).

___ Speaking loudly
___ Talking about feelings
___ Asking a lot of questions
___ Using aggressive body language
___ Talking about cars
___ Talking about sports like baseball, boxing, or football
___ Whispering quietly to another person
___ Playing with hair

___ Wearing perfume
___ Knitting or sewing
___ Painting fingernails or toenails
___ Reading a romance novel
___ Carrying a handbag
___ Opening a door for a member of the opposite sex
___ Crying in public

Other (your own example) _____

Academic Lectures and Note Taking

4 Academic Listening and Note Taking

In this section, you will hear and take notes on a two-part lecture given by Dedra Smith, a media expert who conducts workshops about media and society. The title of the lecture is "Dangers of the Mass Media." Ms. Smith will describe what she believes are some harmful effects of the media today.

> The full-color **design mirrors university textbooks**, providing students with an **authentic university experience.**

BEFORE THE LECTURE

1 Personalizing the topic ⑤

A According to experts, Americans spend a lot of time online. Some people say they spend up to 8 hours a day! What are people doing online? Look at the following chart produced by the Nielsen Company, which monitors media use.

If all U.S. Internet time were condensed into one hour, how much time would be spent in the most heavily used sectors?

- Social Networks/ Blogs 13m 36s
- *Other 20m 36s
- Games 6m 6s
- E-mail 5m 00s
- Portals 2m 36s
- Instant Messaging 2m 24s
- Videos/ Movies 2m 18s
- Search 2m 00s
- Software Info 1m 42s
- Multi-category Entertainment 1m 42s
- Classifieds/ Auctions 1m 36s

*Other includes the 74 remaining online sectors visited from PCs and laptops

Source: Nielsen; data from August 2010

B Work with a partner. Discuss how you spend your time online. Do you spend more or less time on the activities listed above than the typical Internet user?

2 Organizing your notes as a map Ⓝ Ⓛ

One way of taking notes is called *mapping*. In this method, you write the main idea on your paper and draw lines out to related points. As you take notes, you can show connections between different parts of the lecture by adding lines.

> Each unit provides extensive instruction and practice in **taking notes**, helping **students succeed** in university courses.

> Academic lectures take place in real college classrooms, complete with interactions between professors and students.

2 Organizing your notes in columns Ⓝ Ⓛ

It is critical that you organize your notes in a format that helps you understand and remember the content of a lecture. You do not always have time to do this while you are listening to the lecture. The notes you take during a lecture are rough notes. But good note takers revise their notes as soon as possible after a lecture. You revise by putting your notes in an appropriate format and making any changes necessary to clarify the information.

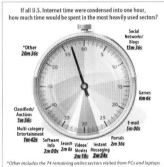

In this book, you will learn several ways to organize your notes. It is important, however, that you experiment and find ways that work best for you. Organizing your notes in columns is one good way to clearly show the difference between main ideas and supporting details.

A Look at these notes on Part 1 of the lecture. Notice that the main ideas are in the left column and the supporting details are in the column on the right.

> Ms. Beth Handman: Family Lessons
> Part One: Rewards and Punishments
>
> | Main Ideas | Details |
> |---|---|
> | 1. Type of family (traditional or nontraditional) is not as important as love and support at home. | • _____
 • _____ |
> | 2. Three ways children learn social behavior from their families: rewards, punishments, modeling. | • finish homework – then TV
 • _____ |
> | 3. Children learn good behavior through rewards. | • _____
 • _____
 • _____ |
> | 4. Another way children learn to behave is through punishments. | • _____
 • _____ |
> | 5. Rewards and punishments are controversial. | • _____
 • If parents are violent, children may become violent |

🔊 **B** Now watch or listen to Part 1 of the lecture. Take notes on your own paper.

C Use your notes to fill in the missing details in the column on the right.

D Compare the notes you took on your own paper and your completed notes with a partner.

Academic Vocabulary and Oral Presentations

Unit 1 Academic Vocabulary Review

This section reviews the vocabulary from Chapters 1 and 2. Some of the words that you needed to learn to understand the content of this unit are specific to its topics. Other words are more general. They appear across different academic fields and are extremely useful for all students to know. For a complete list of all the Academic Word List words in this book, see the Appendix on pages 181–182.

A Read the sentences and fill in the blanks with a form of the word.

1. **acquire (v), acquired (adj):**
   We know that children _____ some behavior from their family members. Honesty and discipline, for example, are _____ values.

2. **alternative (adj), alternatively (adv):**
   Single-gender education and coeducation are two _____ models of education. _____ , children may even do *homeschooling*.

3. **benefits (n), beneficial (adj):**
   Families provide many _____ to their members. For example, eating with other members of the family is very _____ for children.

4. **clarify (v), clarified (v), clarification (n):**
   When I was in my early twenties, my father _____ my problems with me. This _____ was very helpful. Families often help children _____ their goals.

5. **concentrate (v), concentration (n):**
   My son's teacher says if he develops his _____ , he will do much better in school. I always tell him to _____ on what he's doing, too.

6. **conflict (n), conflicting (adj):**
   When there is a _____ between children and their parents, most experts say that the two parents should not give _____ opinions. That does not help the situation.

7. **conform (v), conforming (n):** _____ to group behavior is not always a good idea. It's important to use your own judgment, even when there is pressure to _____ .

8. **consequence (n), consequently (adv):**
   People are influenced by others around them. As a _____ , they tend to follow the behavior of the group. _____ , when in a new culture, they often feel like "a fish out of water."

9. **controversy (n), controversial (adj):**
   There is always a lot of _____ about the best way to bring up children. Education, teaching values, and dealing with peer pressure are all _____ topics.

10. **cooperates (v), cooperation (n), cooperative (adj):**
    My daughter _____ well with her peers and her siblings. Being _____ is one of the most important things I've tried to teach her. _____ is a key to success.

Unit 1 Academic Vocabulary Review

Academic vocabulary development is **critical to student success**. Each unit includes **intensive vocabulary practice**, including words from the Academic Word List.

Students create **oral presentations**, applying the vocabulary and academic content they study in each unit, and **preparing them to speak in a university classroom**.

Oral Presentation

In academic courses, you will sometimes give oral presentations to a small group about a topic you have researched. Here are some guidelines to keep in mind.

BEFORE THE PRESENTATION

1 Choose a topic

There have been many experiments on group dynamics. Choose one of the following topics that you think will be of interest to your classmates.

1. The **Asch conformity experiments**, in which participants were asked to look at some lines
2. The **Milgram experiment** on people's response to authority figures
3. The phenomenon known as "**six degrees of separation**," which examines social networks
4. The **Robbers Cave experiment,** which studied ways to promote understanding between groups

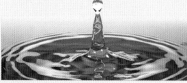

The ripple effect in water.

5. The **ripple effect**, the **domino effect**, and the **butterfly effect**. These expressions are often used to discuss trends and group behavior.

2 Organize your presentation

1. Research your topic in a library or online. Check at least three different Web sites or texts. Be prepared to answer the following questions:
   - When did the experiment take place?
   - Who was involved?
   - What did the researcher(s) do?
   - What did the study show?
2. Plan what you want to say, but do not write it out and memorize it. Instead, make notes on index cards. Plan to speak for no more than 5 minutes.
3. Organize your notes carefully so that you present your ideas clearly. Introduce your topic as soon as you begin speaking.

To the student

Welcome to *Academic Encounters 3 Listening and Speaking: Life in Society*!

The *Academic Encounters* series gets its name because in this series you will *encounter*, or meet, the kinds of *academic* texts (lectures and readings), *academic* language (grammar and vocabulary), and *academic* tasks (taking tests, writing papers, and giving presentations) that you will encounter when you study an academic subject area in English. The goal of the series, therefore, is to prepare you for that encounter.

The approach of *Academic Encounters 3 Listening and Speaking: Life in Society*, may be different from what you are used to in your English studies. In this book, you are asked to study an academic subject area and be responsible for learning that information, in the same way as you might study in a college or university course. You will find that as you study this information, you will at the same time improve your English language proficiency and develop the skills that you will need to be successful when you come to study in your own academic subject area in English.

In *Academic Encounters 3 Listening and Speaking: Life in Society* for example, you will learn:

- what to listen for in academic lectures
- how to think critically about what you have heard
- how to participate in conversations and more formal discussions
- how to give oral presentations in an academic style
- methods of preparing for tests
- strategies for dealing with new vocabulary
- note-taking and study techniques

This course is designed to help you study in English in *any* subject matter. However, because during the study of this book, you will learn a lot of new information about research findings and theories in the field of sociology, you may feel that by the end you have enough background information to one day take and be successful in an introductory course in sociology in English.

We certainly hope that you find *Academic Encounters 3 Listening and Speaking: Life in Society* useful. We also hope that you will find it to be enjoyable. It is important to remember that the most successful learning takes place when you enjoy what you are studying and find it interesting.

Author's acknowledgments

Academic discourse in another language can be both exciting and challenging, and everyone involved in this project has tried to keep students foremost in the design of the exercises. I would like to thank the many people who have supported the development of this series, particularly those whose "behind the scenes" efforts have brought this book into existence.

I thank Bernard Seal, the series editor, whose vision and direction were constantly present. I would like to thank Christopher Sol Cruz, the editorial manager, a source of incredible guidance, and Maya Lazarus, one of the best development editors in the world. Heartfelt thanks also go to the book designers and producers of the audio and video components. Finally, the person who worked with me on the first edition, Kathleen O'Reilly, has been a constant "presence in absence" on the second.

The people who form the centerpiece of the book, namely the interviewees and lecturers, have been amazingly generous in providing me with hours of discussion and expertise. Speaking with you, and hearing your ideas afresh, I am struck by what wonderful people I have been privileged to meet. Last, but not least: Carlos, Kelly, and Victor, as you know, you are my source of inspiration and support.

Kim Sanabria

Publisher's acknowledgments

The first edition of *Academic Encounters* has been used by many teachers in many institutions all around the world. Over the years, countless instructors have passed on feedback about the series, all of which has proven invaluable in helping to direct the vision for the second edition. More formally, a number of reviewers also provided us with a detailed analysis of the series, and we are especially grateful for their insights. We would therefore like to extend particular thanks to the following instructors:

Matthew Gordon Ray Courtney, The University of Auckland, New Zealand

Nancy Hamadou, Pima Community College – West Campus, Tucson, AZ

Yoneko Kanaoka, Hawaii English Language Program at the University of Hawaii at Manoa; Honolulu, Hawaii

Margaret V. Layton, University of Nevada, Reno, Nevada

Dot MacKenzie, Kuwait University, Sabah Al-Salem University City, Kuwait

Jennifer Wharton, Leeward Community College, Pearl City, Hawaii

Unit 1
Belonging to a Group

In this unit, you will hear people discuss what it means to be part of a group. In Chapter 1, you will hear people talk about families and listen to a lecture about how children learn to behave. In Chapter 2, you will consider some of the ways in which individuals are influenced by groups outside the family. You will hear interviews about how the groups we belong to can affect us, and you will listen to a lecture on culture shock.

Contents

In Unit 1, you will listen to and speak about the following topics.

Chapter 1 Marriage, Family, and the Home	Chapter 2 The Power of the Group
Interview 1 Growing Up in a Large Family	**Interview 1** Living With Teenagers
Interview 2 Family Stories	**Interview 2** Expressions About Groups
Lecture Family Lessons	**Lecture** Culture Shock: Group Pressure in Action

Skills

In Unit 1, you will practice the following skills.

Listening Skills	**Speaking Skills**
Listening for factual information Listening for details Listening for stressed words Listening for specific information Listening for main ideas Listening for tone of voice	Sharing your opinion Responding to questions with short answers Asking and answering questions Thinking critically about the topic Personalizing the topic Conducting a survey Studying a syllabus
Vocabulary Skills	**Note Taking Skills**
Reading and thinking about the topic Examining vocabulary in context Guessing vocabulary from context Building background knowledge on the topic	Personalizing the topic Main ideas and supporting details Organizing your notes in columns Organizational phrases Organizing your notes in outline form Copying a lecturer's diagrams and charts

Learning Outcomes

Prepare and **deliver** an oral presentation on an aspect of group dynamics

Chapter 1
Marriage, Family, and the Home

Look at the photographs of families above and answer the questions with a partner.

1. What do these photographs show? In what way are the families you see similar? How are they different?
2. In your opinion, what are some important functions of a family?

1 Getting Started

In this section, you are going to discuss changes in the structure of families. You will also hear information about the average age people get married in different parts of the world.

1 Reading and thinking about the topic

> If you read or think about a topic before you hear it discussed, you will find the discussion much easier to understand.

A Read the following passage:

Over the past century, social changes have dramatically affected the structure of the family. Among these changes are increased industrialization, greater geographical mobility, higher divorce rates, and greater equality for women. Today, in fact, it has become hard to define the word *family*.

Two common family structures in many cultures are the *extended family*, in which many generations live in the same household, and the *nuclear family*, in which two married adults live together with their children. However, both these patterns are now becoming less common.

Today, there are other family structures, such as single-parent families, couples living together without getting married (known as *cohabitation*), divorced couples who remarry, second marriages with children and step-children (known as *blended families*), couples who adopt children, and other different family structures. These structures are becoming more widely accepted. However, although family sizes and structures have changed, the basic functions of a family have remained constant.

B Answer the following questions according to the information in the passage.

1. What changes have affected family structure over the past century?
2. What is meant by the terms *extended family* and *nuclear family*?
3. What are some alternative family structures?

C Read these questions and share your answers with a partner.

1. Have the social changes in the passage affected your own family? If so, how?
2. How would you personally define the word *family*?

2 Sharing your opinion Ⓢ

A Read the list in the left column. It shows some changes that have taken place in the American family during the past century. Work with a partner and fill in the chart with as many positive and negative consequences of these changes as you can. (Some have been done for you.)

Changes in the American family	Positive consequences	Negative consequences
1. Divorce rates in the United States are higher than ever before.	Many people are able to escape from very unhappy relationships.	
2. People are spending much more time at work and less time at home.		Parents spend less time with their children.
3. Compared to a few decades ago, there are many more families where both parents work.		
4. More people are living alone than ever before – up to 25% of all U.S. households.		
5. Almost half the children in the United States spend some time in a single-parent family.		

B Share your ideas with your classmates. In your opinion, are these changes in the family structure harmful to society, or not?

3 Listening for factual information Ⓛ Ⓢ

Listening for factual information is an important skill to practice because conversations, interviews, and lectures often include this type of information. Factual information can include names, numbers, and percentages.

A Look at the flags in the chart below and fill in as many names of countries as you can. Then, with a partner, make predictions about the average age men and women get married in these countries. (Some of the information has already been completed for you.)

	Flag	Country	Average age at which people get married	
			Men	Women
1.			26	24
2.			24	
3.		South Africa		
4.				23
5.				29
6.		United States		
7.				29
8.				
9.			32	
10.		Spain		

B Now listen to the information about the average age people get married around the world. Check your predictions and share your answers with a partner. Did anything surprise you?

2 Real-Life Voices

In this section, you will hear Rickie talk about the reasons families are so important. Then you will hear Charlie, Sheila, and Tina share stories about their families.

BEFORE THE INTERVIEWS

Personalizing the topic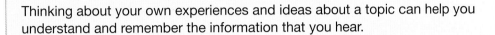

Thinking about your own experiences and ideas about a topic can help you understand and remember the information that you hear.

A Read the following questions and make notes on your answers.

1. How many people were in your immediate household when you were a child? Who were they?
2. How often do you see your family, and on what occasions?
3. What important lessons did you learn from your family members?
4. What is one funny, exciting, strange, or sad story you can share about your family?
5. Is there a particular object that you associate with your family?
6. Which family member would you like to know more about, and why?
7. Does your family have special names (nicknames) for different family members? What are they, and what do they mean?

Families often eat meals together.

B Work with a partner. Share your answers to the questions above.

INTERVIEW 1 Growing Up in a Large Family

1 Examining vocabulary in context

Here are some words and phrases from the interview with Rickie, printed in **bold** and given in the context in which you will hear them. They are followed by definitions.

I come from a pretty big family **by most standards**: *compared to most people*

It's nice to have **home-cooked meals**: *food prepared at home*

Sometimes we fight. But then we usually **make up**: *stop fighting* . . . cousins I **only remotely** remembered: *hardly*

Family **rituals** . . . are great because they remind you of your **roots**: *customs / origins*

. . . basic necessities, like **shelter,** food: *protection, a place to live*

There's . . . a lot of **sibling rivalry** among us: *competition between brothers and sisters*

My sister's kind of **bossy**: domineering: telling others what to do

. . . you also learn how to **compromise**: *give and take, cooperate*

2 Listening for details 🅛 🅢

> Listening for details is an important skill to practice because it will help you improve your listening comprehension. To do this close listening, you have to concentrate and try not to miss any part of what a speaker is saying.

A Read the questions below before you listen to the interview with Rickie.

1. How many children were there in Rickie's household?
   a. three   b. four   c. five

2. Why doesn't Rickie live at home right now?
   a. He's married.   b. He's in college.   c. His parents have moved.

3. Does Rickie get along with his siblings?
   a. No, not really.   b. Yes, usually.   c. Yes, always.

4. What family event does Rickie describe?
   a. a national holiday   b. a birthday   c. a wedding

5. Rickie says that family dinners are important because people . . .
   a. cook together.   b. share their problems.   c. plan the next day.

6. When he began living away, Rickie realized that he didn't know how to . . .
   a. prepare dinner.   b. do the laundry.   c. manage his finances.

7. When Rickie had a problem and felt embarrassed about it, what did he do?
   a. He talked to his friends.   b. He called home.   c. He solved it alone.

8. Rickie used to fight with his brother about . . .
   a. clothes   b. girls   c. toys

🔊 **B** Now listen to the interview with Rickie and circle the correct answer to each question in Step A.

C Compare your answers with a partner.

1 Examining vocabulary in context

Here are some words and phrases from the interview with Charlie, Sheila, and Tina, printed in bold and given in the context in which you will hear them. They are followed by definitions.

My father **distracted** my mother: *entertained, kept her from paying attention to something*

My sister and I were **giggling** so much: *laughing in an uncontrolled way*

It took about two days to even **thaw out**: *defrost*

It's **hysterical**: *really funny*

Tell me about a family **keepsake**: *object that belongs to the family*

It's **unique**: *distinctive, different*

Is it **valuable**?: *worth a lot of money*

It'll be like a family **heirloom**: *an object that remains in the family for many years*

He was the **black sheep** of the family: *a family member with a bad reputation*

2 Responding to questions with short answers Ⓢ Ⓛ Ⓝ

Students are often asked to provide short answers to simple questions. These answers show that the listener understands and can communicate the information he or she has heard.

A Read the following questions before you listen to the interviews with Charlie, Sheila, and Tina.

1. Charlie describes a holiday. Which holiday does he talk about, and how does the family intend to celebrate it?

_____

2. Charlie's father realizes that the family has made a big mistake. What is it?

_____

3. Why does the family want to hide the mistake from Charlie's mother?

_____

4. What happens many years later?

_____

5. What does Sheila's statue look like?

_____

6. What are the two reasons Sheila gives for liking this statue?

_____

7. What does Sheila want to do with the statue in the future?

_____

8. Which family member does Tina talk about?

_____

9. Why is it difficult for her to discuss him?

_____

Many families pass down stories, photos, and other objects from one generation to the next.

🔊 **B** Now listen to the interviews. Listen for the information that you need to answer the questions in Step A while you take notes. Then write complete sentences to respond to the questions.

C Compare your answers with a partner. They do not have to be exactly the same.

3 Listening for stressed words 🅛 🅢

When speakers want to stress an idea, they often stress a particular word in the sentence by saying it louder or more slowly. Look at these examples:

I **LOVE** my sister. (the speaker stresses the fact that he really cares for his sister)
I love my **SISTER**. (the speaker cares for his sister in particular, but may not care so much for other family members)

A Look at the chart before you listen to excerpts from the interview.

Excerpts	Which word does the speaker stress?	What does the speaker mean?
1. "I'm not living at home anymore, and I really miss everybody."	a. miss b. everybody	c. He is very sad. d. He would like to be with each one of his family members.
2. "Mom always tried to make sure that we sat down and ate together."	a. always b. tried	c. His mom constantly organized family dinners. d. His mom was not successful in her efforts.
3. "We've always had problems cooking the turkey."	a. cooking b. turkey	c. The family had difficulty with the turkey in particular. d. The family had no difficulty preparing the food, just cooking it.
4. "I always wanted to play with the bowl."	a. play b. bowl	c. She wanted to play games. d. The bowl was what interested her, not the other items.
5. "My uncle works in tourism, and I think he travels a lot."	a. think b. lot	c. She knows her uncle travels, and she believes he travels often. d. She's not sure if her uncle travels.

🔊 **B** Now listen to the excerpts. Circle the correct responses in each column and compare your answers with a partner.

Thinking critically about the topic Ⓢ

> Make it a habit to evaluate what other people say and compare it with your own knowledge and experiences.

A Are the experiences of Rickie, Charlie, Sheila, and Tina similar to yours, or are they different? Check (✓) the appropriate column. Then explain your answers to a partner.

Experiences of Rickie, Charlie, Sheila, and Tina	Your Experience	
	Similar	Different
Rickie		
Has many siblings	☐	☐
Spent important occasions with his extended family	☐	☐
Regularly ate dinner with his family	☐	☐
Found it hard to begin to live alone	☐	☐
Charlie		
Has memories about funny family events	☐	☐
Enjoys remembering family secrets	☐	☐
Sheila		
Can easily identify one family keepsake	☐	☐
Was taught to value her possessions	☐	☐
Tina		
Has a family member she hasn't seen for a long time	☐	☐
Remembers a conflict in her family	☐	☐

B Work with a partner. Write one question you would like to ask Rickie, Charlie, Sheila, or Tina about their families. Try to imagine how the interviewees might respond. Role-play the questions and answers with your partner.

3 In Your Own Voice

In this section you will practice asking and answering questions about wedding customs. Divide the class into two groups: Group A and Group B. Group A, follow the directions below. Group B, go to the next page and follow the directions there.

Asking and answering questions: Group A Ⓢ

A Read the information about weddings around the world. You will need to tell other students about these facts and customs, so make sure you understand them and can pronounce all the words clearly.

Weddings Around the World

In Russia, couples release white birds into the air just before they get married.

Las Vegas is called the "wedding capital of the world."

"Blackening," or "blackening the bride," is a Scottish custom that involves covering the bride, or bride and groom, with sauces and feathers.

According to tradition, couples are supposed to put coins in their shoes before they get married.

In Holland, people often give the gift of flower bulbs to newlyweds.

In Greece, newlyweds eat olives to celebrate their marriage.

B Look at the grid and try to answer the questions. Practice reading the questions aloud.

In China, what do couples exchange before they get married?	What do wedding guests sometimes throw at a newly married couple in the United States?	What do women in India sometimes wear on their face to show they are married?
In Germany, what do couples break before they get married?	According to American custom, you are supposed to give a bride four things to wear on her wedding day. What are they?	In the United States, women throw their flower bouquets over their head. Why?

C Now work with a partner from Group B. Take turns asking your partner the questions in the grid, in whatever order you like. (Group B has different questions to ask.) When your partner asks you a question, listen carefully. Then use the information you read in Step A to answer the questions.

Asking and answering questions: Group B ⑤

A Read the information about weddings around the world. You will need to tell other students these facts and customs, so make sure you understand them and can pronounce all the words clearly.

Weddings Around the World

In China, couples often exchange red handkerchiefs at their wedding. The handkerchiefs are symbols of a long, happy life together.

When couples get married, the guests often throw confetti (paper), rice, or other food at them. This practice will bring the couples good luck.

In India, brides often wear a bindi (red dot) or red color in their hair to show they are married.

In Germany and other countries, couples often break dishes and plates before the wedding.

According to U.S. custom, you are supposed to give a new bride something old, something new, something borrowed, and something blue.

When American brides throw their bouquets over their heads, unmarried women try to catch them so that they can get married, too.

B Look at the grid and try to answer the questions. Practice reading the questions aloud.

In Russia, what do couples do before they get married so that they will have good luck?	Where is the wedding capital of the world?	In Scotland, there is a wedding custom called "blackening." What does it involve?
What are couples supposed to put in their shoes before they get married?	What gift is often given to newlyweds in Holland?	In which country do newlyweds eat olives to celebrate their marriage?

C Now work with a partner from Group A. Take turns asking your partner the questions in the grid, in whatever order you like. (Group A has different questions to ask.) When your partner asks you a question, listen carefully. Then use the information you read in Step A to answer the questions.

4 Academic Listening and Note Taking

In this section, you will hear and take notes on a two-part lecture given by Ms. Beth Handman, an educational consultant. The title of the lecture is "Family Lessons." Ms. Handman will explain how children learn lessons within a family, no matter what type of family they come from.

BEFORE THE LECTURE

1 Personalizing the topic Ⓝ Ⓢ

A Work with a partner. Read the seven examples of bad behavior in children listed below. Discuss the best and worst ways for parents to react to each of these behaviors. The "best way" means a way that is likely to teach good behavior to the child. The "worst way" is a way that will probably not be successful in teaching good behavior. Make brief notes about your ideas.

1. Sarah, a two-year-old, keeps throwing her food on the floor and cries until her parents pick it up.

   Best way to react: _____

   Worst way to react: _____

2. David, a five-year-old, is angry and frustrated. He hits his baby sister.

   Best way to react: _____

   Worst way to react: _____

3. Ronnie, a six-year-old, runs up and down the aisles when his parents take him to the supermarket and screams when they tell him to stop.

   Best way to react: _____

   Worst way to react: _____

4. Sheila, an I l-year-old, is caught copying a classmate's test.

   Best way to react: _____

   Worst way to react: _____

5. Stephen, a 12-year-old, takes money from his father's wallet.

   Best way to react: _____

   Worst way to react: _____

6. Tim, a 13-year-old, begins to smoke cigarettes.

   Best way to react: _____

   Worst way to react: _____

7. Erica, a 15-year-old, refuses to go to bed until 2 a.m.

   Best way to react: _____

   Worst way to react: _____

B Using your notes, compare your answers with other classmates.

To state your opinion, use:

I think / I believe / I feel . . .
In my opinion, . . .
To make a recommendation, use:
Parents should / You could / We ought to . . .

Example

A: I think that Sarah wants to get attention. The best thing is to stop paying attention to her when she throws her food on the floor.

B: I disagree with you. Remember, Sarah is only two years old. I think she needs her parents' attention. Ignoring her is the worst way to react.

2 Main ideas and supporting details Ⓝ Ⓛ

The first step in listening to a lecture and taking notes is to try to distinguish between the lecturer's main ideas and the supporting details. A supporting detail often consists of:

- an example, such as a story or anecdote
- an academic reference, such as the definition of a term, some statistics, the name of a researcher, or reference to a research study

Speakers may introduce supporting details with the following phrases:

For instance,	**X can be defined as . . .**
For example,	**According to a recent study, . . .**
Let me give you an example . . .	**It has been estimated that . . .**

A Watch or listen. You will hear a few sentences from the lecture about each of the main ideas listed below. Decide whether these supporting details are examples or academic references. Put a check (✓) in the appropriate column.

Main Ideas	Supporting Details	
	Example	Academic reference
1. Children learn good behavior through rewards.	☐	☐
2. Another way children learn to behave is through punishments.	☐	☐
3. Parents can teach children by modeling appropriate behavior.	☐	☐
4. "Don't do as I do; do as I tell you" doesn't usually work.	☐	☐
5. Parents worry about negative lessons.	☐	☐

B Compare your answers with a partner.

1 Guessing vocabulary from context Ⓥ

When you hear or read words that you do not know, pay attention to the words in the surrounding context. The context can give you clues that will help you understand the new words. Using your knowledge of related words will also help you.

A Read the conversation between Dr. P., a child psychologist, and some young parents. Dr. P. is talking about ways to teach children the lessons they need to learn.

Dr. P.: It's very important to be aware of the way we behave around young people because children (a) <u>learn</u> both good and bad behavior from the people around them: they are (b) <u>taught how to behave</u> by everyone they know.

Mother: How can we make sure our children develop good habits?

Dr. P.: Well, another way is to give them rewards. For example, if you want your child to stop biting his nails, you can try giving him cookies or candy when he doesn't bite them. Giving the child a candy is a reward, a kind of (c) "<u>carrot</u>," but I think it works. It's a way to (d) <u>strengthen</u> good behavior. And rewards don't have to be big. Even a smile can help a child behave well, and this is the kind of reward that you probably give (e) <u>even without thinking</u>.

Father: We think children should have (f) <u>responsibilities</u>, but they don't always do what we tell them to do.

Dr. P.: When I grew up, my parents used to (g) <u>hit</u> me if I misbehaved, or even if I (h) <u>spoke impolitely</u> to them. But personally, I don't agree with this approach. I consider it a form of (i) <u>extreme cruelty</u>. Most parents think children need to do what their parents ask, but punishment is a topic that is very (j) <u>difficult for people to agree about</u>.

B Work with a partner. Match each of the words in the list with an underlined item in the advice column in Step A. Write the letter on the line. Check your answers in a dictionary if necessary.

1. abuse _____
2. acquire _____
3. bribe _____
4. controversial _____
5. duties _____

6. spank _____
7. reinforce _____
8. socialized _____
9. talked back _____
10. unconsciously _____

2 Organizing your notes in columns

It is critical that you organize your notes in a format that helps you understand and remember the content of a lecture. You do not always have time to do this while you are listening to the lecture. The notes you take during a lecture are rough notes. But good note takers revise their notes as soon as possible after a lecture. You revise by putting your notes in an appropriate format and making any changes necessary to clarify the information.

In this book, you will learn several ways to organize your notes. It is important, however, that you experiment and find ways that work best for you. Organizing your notes in columns is one good way to clearly show the difference between main ideas and supporting details.

A Look at these notes on Part 1 of the lecture. Notice that the main ideas are in the left column and the supporting details are in the column on the right.

Ms. Beth Handman: Family Lessons
Part One: Rewards and Punishments

Main Ideas	Details
1. Type of family (traditional or nontraditional) is not as important as love and support at home.	• _____ • _____ • _____
2. Three ways children learn social behavior from their families: rewards, punishments, modeling.	• finish homework – then TV • _____ • _____
3. Children learn good behavior through rewards.	• _____ • _____ • _____
4. Another way children learn to behave is through punishments.	• _____ • _____
5. Rewards and punishments are controversial.	• _____ • _____ • If parents are violent, children may become violent

 B Now watch or listen to Part 1 of the lecture. Take notes on your own paper.

 C Use your notes to fill in the missing details in the column on the right.

D Compare the notes you took on your own paper and your completed notes with a partner.

1 Guessing vocabulary from context Ⓥ

A The following items contain important vocabulary from Part 2 of the lecture. Work with a partner. Using the context and your knowledge of related words, take turns guessing the meanings of the words in **bold**.

1. ___ Children's first **role models** are their parents.

2. ___ Parents can **set a good example** for children.

3. ___ There is an old **saying** in English: "Don't do as I do; do as I tell you." But this advice doesn't work most of the time.

4. ___ If you smoke yourself, it is probably **ineffective** to tell a child not to smoke.

5. ___ Many people do not even realize the **impact** that they can have on a child.

6. ___ It is common for babysitters, relatives, and **child-care centers** to take care of children.

7. ___ The most important thing for children is to grow up in an environment where there are fair rules that are clearly established and followed **consistently** by everyone.

B Work with your partner. Match the vocabulary terms with their definitions. Write the letter of each definition next to the sentence containing the correct term in Step A. Check your answers in a dictionary if necessary.

a. influence

b. not useful

c. in the same way all the time

d. show (others) how to behave

e. proverb

f. people who are an example for them to copy

g. places where professionals take care of young children

2 Organizing your notes in columns Ⓝ Ⓛ

A Look at these notes on Part 2 of the lecture. Notice that the first main idea is number 6 because the last main idea in Part 1 was number 5.

Ms. Beth Handman: Family Lessons

Part Two: Modeling

Main Ideas   Details

6. Modeling means _____
_____.

7. _____   • _____

8. "Don't do as I do, _____ "   • _____
doesn't work.   • _____

9. Modeling is the most important   • Children have many models:
way children learn.   _____ , _____ ,
                                                babysitters, professionals in
                                                child-care centers, each other, TV

10. Parents worry about negative   • _____
lessons   • _____

11. Most important thing: _____
_____
_____

🔊 **B** Now watch or listen to Part 2 of the lecture. Take notes on your own paper.

👥 **C** Use your notes to fill in the missing main ideas and details in the columns.

D Compare the notes you took on your own paper and your completed notes with a partner.

Sharing your opinion ⓢ

An issue becomes more interesting if you share your own opinion about it. Your ideas will probably be influenced by many factors, including your age, educational experience, and cultural background. It is likely that people with backgrounds different from yours will have different opinions.

A Read the list of behavior, skills, and values that children should learn. With a partner, fill in the chart with your ideas. How should children learn these lessons? Who should teach them? At what age should they learn them?

What children should learn		How?	Who?	At what age?
Good behavior	Avoiding junk food			
	Saying "please" and "thank you"			
	Cleaning up after an activity			
	Other behavior (you choose) _____			
Skills	Playing a musical instrument			
	Reading and writing well			
	Learning a foreign language			
	Other important skill (you choose) _____			
Values	Responsibility			
	Self-discipline			
	Caring for others			
	Other important value (you choose) _____			

B As a class, share the results of your discussions about child-care arrangements and the behavior, skills, and values children should learn. Compare your answers. You can use these phrases in your discussion:

I am sure that . . .   I am concerned about . . .
I strongly believe that . . .   The problem is that . . .
I am convinced that . . .   The main advantage is that . . .
I worry that . . .   A disadvantage might be that . . .

Chapter 2
The Power of the Group

Look at the photographs of different groups and answer the questions with a partner.

> **1.** What groups do you see in these photographs? What groups do you belong to?
>
> **2.** What are the benefits of belonging to a group? What are the disadvantages?

1 Getting Started

In this section, you are going to discuss the groups you belong to and how groups influence behavior. You will also hear two college students discuss group pressure and compare their ideas with your own.

1 Reading and thinking about the topic Ⓥ Ⓢ

A Read the following passage.

As individuals in society, each of us belongs to several different groups. For example, we are members of our own families, we have groups of friends, and we associate with groups at work, at school, and maybe in religious settings. Group membership seems to be a basic human instinct. Each group has its own culture, or set of rules that governs the behavior of people in that group.

In fact, groups often influence the behavior of individuals. We may think that we act alone, but in fact there are always group pressures that influence us to act in certain ways. It is common for *peers* – people of the same age or people in the same situation – to behave in similar ways or to share similar expectations. Peer pressure is especially strong during adolescence, so parents of teenagers often worry about the influence that friends have on their children.

We also belong to larger groups, like our society or nation. Many sociologists believe that cultures can be divided into *individualist* and *collectivist* models. Individualist cultures place more emphasis on the individual, and people are expected to develop their own opinions and affiliations. In collectivist cultures, on the other hand, people act mostly as members of a group. Wherever we are born and grow up, the groups we belong to influence our opinions about the world, our interactions with others, and the decisions we make.

B Answer the following questions according to the information in the passage.

1. What are some groups that an individual can belong to?

2. What is peer pressure?

3. In what ways does belonging to a group influence our behavior?

C Read these questions and share your answers with a partner.

1. Do you belong to any groups other than the ones mentioned in the passage? Explain.

2. Can you think of a time when group pressure made you act in a certain way? Describe it to your partner.

3. Which do you think your culture emphasizes more – the individual or the group?

2 Sharing your opinion Ⓢ Ⓥ

A Work with a partner and read the quotes below. Look up words you do not understand. Then, in your own words, discuss what you think each quote means.

1. "Snowflakes, leaves, humans, plants, raindrops, stars, molecules, microscopic entities all come in communities. The singular cannot in reality exist."
Paula Gunn Allen, 1939–2008, Native American poet

2. "Solitary trees grow strong."
Winston Churchill, 1874–1965, British politician

3. "Talent wins games, but teamwork and intelligence win championships."
Michael Jordan, 1963–, American basketball star

4. "We cannot live only for ourselves. A thousand fibers connect us with our fellow men."
Herman Melville, 1819–1891, American novelist

5. "For every one of us that succeeds, it's because there's somebody there to show you the way."
Oprah Winfrey, 1954–, American talk show personality

B Do you think each idea above emphasizes individuals or groups? Discuss with your partner.

3 Listening for specific information 🅛 🅢

As a student, you will often need to answer questions about specific information that you have heard. Preview the questions before you listen so that you know what information to listen for.

A Read these questions about "group pressure" situations.

1. You have been invited to the wedding of a family member you don't like. Everyone else in your family is going. Would you go to the wedding?

2. Your friends are planning to see a popular movie this weekend and have asked you to go with them. You have read reviews that say it is a really bad movie. Would you go with your friends anyway?

3. All your friends have started to wear a new style of shoes. When you first see the shoes, you think they look ugly. Would you consider buying them anyway?

4. Your parents have been invited to their friend's house in the country for the weekend. They want you to go with them. You are in college and need to study. Would you go away with your parents for the weekend?

5. You are looking for a job, and your mother's friend says she can help. Would you accept her offer?

B Listen to two college students – Rebecca and Jim. What do they say they would do in these situations? Take notes about their answers.

Situation	Rebecca's response	Jim's response
1. Going to a relative's wedding		
2. Going to a movie		
3. Buying new shoes		
4. Going away for the weekend		
5. Finding a job		

C Compare your answers in a small group. Do any of Rebecca's or Jim's reasons for their answers surprise you? Discuss what you would do in these situations.

2 Real-Life Voices

In this section, you will hear two people discuss group membership and group pressure. First, you will hear Henry, the father of two adolescent boys, talk about peer pressure. Then you will hear Grace discuss expressions related to group membership.

BEFORE THE INTERVIEWS

Sharing your opinion ⓢ

A Work with a partner and read the comments, made by adolescents, below. How do you think their parents should respond, and why? Write some possible responses below each comment.

1. Girl, 12: All my friends are getting tattoos, and I want to get one, too. I was thinking of getting a big dragon on my back.

_____

2. Boy, 13: I'm going to get my ear pierced. Just the left one. I think that looks really cool.

_____

3. Girl, 14: My friend showed me a hair dye that you can use yourself, and I'm thinking of getting some. I'm not sure whether to choose blue or orange.

_____

4. Boy, 15: Look, I'll get to my homework later. I just want to check out this video game for a while.

_____

5. Girl, 16: I'm not that hungry, so I don't need dinner. I'll just be in my room talking online. I'll get something to eat later.

_____

6. Boy, 17: Don't wait up for me tonight. I know it's only Tuesday, but I'm going out tonight, and I won't be home until about midnight.

_____

B Read the conversations between teenage children and their family members below. Match each bold expression with its meaning. Write the number below.

1. Son: I have to go to soccer practice later on, but I'm feeling upset because I feel like I never get to kick the ball.

Dad: Well, soccer is a team game, and the point is to try to support each other. Just remember, **there's no "I" in team!**

2. Daughter: I'm going to get my hair cut really short. I saw a woman actor with that hairstyle on TV, and it looks really great on some of my friends at school. What do you think?

Dad: Well, think carefully before you do that. Just because **everyone else is jumping on the bandwagon**, it doesn't mean that you have to.

3. Son: I might do my homework at my friend's house this evening. We work well together.

Mother: That's fine. I think you should be working together. You know what they say: **Two heads are better than one**!

4. Daughter: I'm feeling stressed about my college application.

Father: Try not to worry too much. How are your friends handling their applications? After all, **you're all in the same boat**.

5. Grandson: I'm not sure what to wear at my school event this weekend.

Grandfather: Well, just **go along with the crowd.** What are other people wearing?

6. Niece: My friend just installed some software on her computer, and now it's crashed. I told her not to do that.

Aunt: Well, you have to let people make their own mistakes. **Don't be a backseat driver.**

a. ___ Do what everyone else is doing.

b. ___ People are doing the same thing, following the crowd.

c. ___ Working in pairs is more successful than working alone.

d. ___ It is important to work together and cooperate with others.

e. ___ Don't try to control other people.

f. ___ You are in the same situation.

INTERVIEW 1   Living with Teenagers

1 Examining vocabulary in context Ⓥ

Here are some words and phrases from the interview with Henry, printed in **bold** and given in the context in which you will hear them. They are followed by definitions.

Group pressure can strongly affect adolescents.

> Adolescence is the time when the pressure begins to **shift**: *move or change*
>
> **. . . comes into full bloom** at about 13, 14: *becomes fully developed*
>
> You can tell **at a glance**: *with a quick look*
>
> **. . .** with the hope that the **fad** would have passed: *a new fashion that is suddenly popular*

Should you be trying to **monitor it**?: *watch it carefully*

Where you **draw the line**: *place a limit on what is permitted*

Parents always worry that their kids will get **bullied**: *intimidated, frightened by others*

Kids . . . join **cliques**: *groups of friends with shared interests*

They are real **copycats**, and they tend to listen to the same thing: *people who copy others' behavior*

2 Listening for main ideas ⒧ Ⓢ

> Informal interviews and conversations are usually less organized than lectures and presentations. So, when you want to understand the main ideas, you have to think back over the whole interview or conversation and try to figure out what the people were trying to express.

A In this interview, Henry gives advice about how to deal with teenage children. Before you listen, read the following advice that is commonly given to parents on this subject.

Advice to Parents on How to Deal with Teenage Children

1. ___ Be a good role model. Show them how to behave well by behaving well yourself.

2. ___ Let them make their own decisions about fashion when they are ready.

3. ___ Monitor their behavior.

4. ___ Give them freedom to experiment and have fun, as long as their behavior is safe and legal.

5. ___ Discuss everything with your children.

6. ___ Set clear limits. Be clear about what they can and cannot do.

7. ___ Listen to the way you talk to them. Avoid the annoying language that your own parents used with you.

8. ___ Leave your children alone. Trust that they will ask you for advice if and when they need it.

9. ___ Make sure you know who your children's friends are.

🔊 **B** Now listen. Check (✓) the main ideas from the list above that Henry discusses.

C Discuss the following questions with a partner.

1. Do you agree with Henry's advice?

2. What do you think Henry's sons think about his approach?

3. Did your parents or family members act in a similar way to Henry when you were growing up? How?

Many cultures emphasize the identity of the group.

1 Examining vocabulary in context Ⓥ

Here are some words and phrases from the interview with Grace, printed in **bold** and given in the context in which you will hear them. They are followed by definitions.

I immigrated as a **graduate student**: *student studying for an advanced degree, like an MA*

. . . there's more **emphasis** on doing what the family thinks: *stress, focus on the importance of*

I'm a **linguist**: *a person specializing in languages*

I learned the proverb "**Birds of a feather flock together**": *people who are similar do similar things together*

You tend to **hang out with** people who are like you: *spend time with*

That expression deals with **conformity**: *acting in the same way as other people*

They flocked to the concert in droves: *large numbers of people went to the concert*

The expression **implies** that you should not copy other people: *suggests*

2 Listening for specific information Ⓛ Ⓢ

🔊 **A** Read the questions below. Then listen to the interview with Grace. Answer as many questions as you can. Compare your answers with a partner.

1. Where is Grace originally from?
   a. China
   b. Japan

2. How long has Grace been living in the United States?
   a. for nearly 12 years
   b. for over 20 years

3. What are two topics that Grace disagrees with Henry about?
   a. clothes and music
   b. hairstyles and computers

4. Grace is interested in an idiom about a number. Which number is it?
   a. one
   b. ten

5. Grace thinks the expression about sheep shows that
   a. people don't think for themselves.
   b. people admire strong leaders.

6. Which animals travel in "droves"?
   a. cats and dogs
   b. cows and horses

7. The Japanese expression that Grace discusses means that
   a. you should try to be different from other people.
   b. you should try to be similar to other people.

🔊 **B** Now listen to the interview again. Check your answers and correct the ones that you got wrong.

3 Listening for tone of voice 🅛 🅢

🔊 **A** Listen again to excerpts from the interviews. Check (✓) the column that describes the speaker's tone.

	The speaker is serious.	The speaker is joking.
1. Henry is discussing fashion choices.		
2. Henry is discussing a fad.		
3. Henry is discussing his attitude.		
4. Grace is discussing her culture.		
5. Grace is discussing an expression.		

B With a partner, compare your responses.

AFTER THE INTERVIEWS

Personalizing the topic 🅢

Discuss the following questions with a partner. Give as much information as you can. Then share your ideas with the class.

When you were an adolescent:

1. Did your family try to influence the clothes you wore?

2. Did you ever have friends that your family did not like?

3. What time did you have to be home in the evening?

4. Were you allowed to date?

5. Did you spend a lot of time alone?

6. Did your family have strict rules about what you couldn't do?

7. Did your family worry about cliques or bullies?

8. Were you encouraged to follow others' examples or to think for yourself?

9. Were your parents' rules different from the rules of your friends' parents?

3 In Your Own Voice

In this section, you will discuss some ways that ideas spread among groups. Then you will conduct a short survey to find out what other people think about recent trends and share your findings with the class.

1 Thinking critically about the topic ⓢ

A Read the following passage.

Many writers are interested in the actions of groups of people. In his book, *The Tipping Point*, best-selling author Malcolm Gladwell explains how he thinks successful ideas, behaviors, and products spread. One of his main points is that three basic types of people are responsible for spreading any particular trend. Together, these people play an important role in how the rest of us think and act.

- Person A is the kind of person who connects other people together.
- Person B is the specialist who provides other people with new information.
- Person C is the kind of person who makes others believe his or her message.

B With a small group, answer the questions below.

1. Have you read *The Tipping Point*? If not, would you like to?
2. Do you know people like Gladwell's A, B, and C? For example, do you have any friends who seem to know everyone? Do you know someone who always seems to be aware of the latest news or trends? Do you know anyone who is very good at making others agree with him or her? Tell your partners about these people.
3. Give an example of an idea, political movement, habit, fashion, book, movie, or something else that seems to have suddenly become popular. How do you explain this popularity?

2 Conducting a survey ⓢ ⓝ

> Collecting ideas from your friends and other people that you know can make it really interesting to discuss a topic. Conducting your own survey may give you ideas that you had not thought of before.

A Fads usually become popular very suddenly and then go away suddenly, too. Interview three people outside your class about recent fads. Try to find people of different ages and backgrounds. Here is a way to start the interview:

Hi. I'm doing a survey for my English class about fads. Could you spare me a few minutes? This shouldn't take very long. If you don't mind, I'll take notes as you speak so that I can remember everything you say.
Can you tell me about a fashion item that is particularly popular these days?
And what about a food or drink item that is particularly popular at the moment?

B Take brief notes on what the people say as you interview them. Write your notes in this chart. Also write down the sex and approximate age of each person you interview in case this becomes important.

Survey About Fads			
	Person 1	**Person 2**	**Person 3**
Sex:			
Age:			
Items That Are Particularly Popular at the Moment			
A fashion item:			
A food or drink:			
A game or sport:			
A musician or entertainer:			
A book, movie, or TV show:			
A Web site or YouTube video:			

C Now share your findings about recent fads with a small group or with the class. Discuss why you believe these fads exist and how long they will last. Can Gladwell's list of three important people help you understand the popularity of these fads?

4 Academic Listening and Note Taking

In this section, you will hear and take notes on a two-part lecture given by Iván Zatz, a professor of social sciences and cross-cultural studies. The lecture title is "Culture Shock: Group Pressure in Action." Professor Zatz will explain why and how culture shock occurs.

1 Building background knowledge on the topic

> When you attend a lecture, you almost always know what the topic will be. It is a good idea to do some background reading on the topic first so that you can become familiar with some of the terms and ideas that are likely to be discussed by the lecturer.

A Before you hear the lecture on culture shock, it will be helpful to think about the concept of *culture.* Read the following passage about culture.

> *Culture* has been defined as "everything humans are socialized to do, think, use, and make." In 1966, Edward Hall compared the nature of culture to an iceberg. You can see part of an iceberg, but most of the iceberg is below the water and cannot be seen. Similarly, most aspects of culture are not visible. These invisible aspects are things that we are familiar with but don't usually think about or question.
>
> An example of an aspect of culture that is visible – one that is *above* the water level – would be the type of jobs that people have. In other words, the types of jobs may differ from culture to culture, and this is a subject that people commonly discuss. An example of an invisible cultural aspect – one that is *below* the water level – would be ways of being polite or impolite. Everyone in a society knows what behavior is polite or impolite, but they don't often think about it consciously or question it.

B Read the list of aspects of culture. For each aspect, decide if it would be above or below the water level of the cultural iceberg and write it on an appropriate line in the illustration on page 33.

- ways of showing emotion
- our ideas about what looks fashionable
- the ways older and younger people should behave
- the amount of physical distance we leave between ourselves and others when we have a conversation
- names of popular musicians
- our ideas about what looks beautiful
- the kind of food that is sold in supermarkets
- how late we can arrive at an appointment without being rude

ABOVE the water level: cultural aspects that are easy to identify and discuss

BELOW the water level: cultural aspects that are commonly understood but are not usually questioned

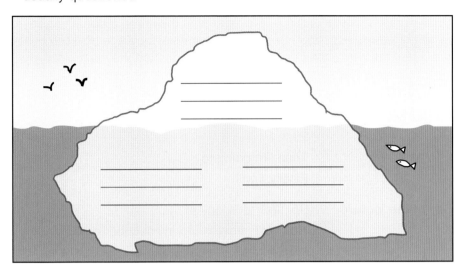

C Compare your ideas in a small group. Then, with your group, add other items that you think should go above and below the water level.

2 Studying a syllabus ⓢ

Many professors hand out a syllabus that includes a brief description of each of the lectures for the course. If you study the syllabus before a lecture and think about the possible content of the lecture you are going to hear, it will make the lecture easier to follow.

A Read the following description from Professor Zatz's syllabus.

> Week 6: Culture Shock – Group Pressure in Action
>
> - Definition of culture shock   - Stages of culture shock
>
> - Reasons for culture shock   - Practical applications of research

B Work with a partner. Look up the definition of *culture shock* in a dictionary and copy it down.

_____

C Discuss the following questions with your partner.

1. Why do you think people experience culture shock?
2. How do you think people who have culture shock feel?
3. Do you think that culture shock can be avoided? How?

D Compare your answers with the class.

3 Organizational phrases Ⓝ Ⓛ

Good lecturers make it easy to understand and take notes on their lectures by using organizational phrases. These phrases may appear in the introduction, the body of the lecture, or the conclusion. You need to listen carefully for these phrases because they will show you the way the lecture is organized and when the main ideas are going to be introduced. Here are some examples of typical phrases:

In the introduction	Today, I'm going to talk about . . .
	First, I will . . .
	Then I'm going to . . .
	Finally, I will . . .
In the body of the lecture	So, first, let's look at . . .
	Now let's move on to my second topic, which is . . .
	Finally, I want you to consider . . .
In the conclusion	Let me summarize for you . . .
	So, the three main points that we have examined today are . . .

A The organizational phrases below are from the lecture. Work out the order in which you think they will appear. Write *1* next to the phrase that you think will come first in the lecture, *2* next to the second phrase, and so on.

a. ___ Now let's turn to . . .

b. ___ I'm going to focus on three main ideas in this lecture . . .

c. ___ Secondly, I will describe . . .

d. ___ The subject of today's lecture is . . .

e. ___ To conclude, let's look at . . .

f. ___ First of all, we will consider . . .

g. ___ Finally, I'll mention . . .

h. ___ First, then, . . .

B Compare your answers with a partner.

C Now, listen to these phrases in the order that they actually appear in the lecture and note which comes first, second, third, and so on. Write the letter in the correct blank below.

1. ___   2. ___   3. ___   4. ___   5. ___   6. ___   7. ___   8. ___

1 Guessing vocabulary from context Ⓥ

Work with a partner. The column on the left contains important vocabulary from Part 1 of the lecture. Using the context and your knowledge of related words, complete the blanks in the chart with the vocabulary words. The first one has been done for you.

1. articulated 2. complex 3. govern 4. immense 5. irrationally 6. manifestation 7. phenomenon 8. stressful 9. surroundings	**a.** People are often influenced by the environment around them, or their _____ .	**b.** The lecturer discussed culture shock. He <u>articulated</u> his ideas clearly.	**c.** The way our peers behave and think has a(n) _____ impact on our own behavior.
	d. When people move to a different country, everything changes. This experience can be very _____ .	**e.** Societies are not easy to understand. They are very _____ .	**f.** He did not really think about what he was doing. He acted _____ .
	g. There are unspoken rules that _____ our behavior, whether we like it or not.	**h.** When she feels stressed, she argues with her family. That's just a(n) _____ of her feelings.	**i.** The _____ of culture shock affects most visitors to another country.

2 Organizing your notes in outline form Ⓝ Ⓛ

An outline is a traditional format for organizing notes in English-speaking countries. In a formal outline, main points are usually indicated as Roman numerals (I, II, III, etc.). Under each main point there are usually supporting points – or details – that are indicated as capital letters (A B, C, etc.). Underneath these are Arabic numerals (1, 2, 3, etc.).

Remember that you may not be able to organize your notes in the best way while you are listening to a lecture. But you should revise your notes as soon after the lecture as possible.

A Look at the outline of Part 1 of the lecture. Think about what kind of information you might need to complete the outline.

> Professor Ivan Zatz
>   Culture Shock – Group Pressure in Action
> I. Definition of culture shock = _____
> II. 3 main ideas
>   A. _____
>   B. _____
>   C. Applications of culture-shock research
> III. Reasons for culture shock
>   A. one set of rules growing up – not often articulated
>   B. other countries – _____
>   C. can't use your own _____
>   1. people act _____
>   2. people feel _____

B Now watch or listen to Part 1 of the lecture. Take notes on your own paper.

C Use your notes to complete the outline in Step A.

D Compare the notes you took and your completed outline for Step A with a partner.

LECTURE PART 2   Stages of Culture Shock

1 Guessing vocabulary from context **V**

A The following items contain important vocabulary from Part 2 of the lecture. Work with a partner. Using the context and your knowledge of related words, take turns guessing the meanings of the words in **bold.**

1. ___ If you were to **depict** it on paper, you might draw a "wave" shape.

2. ___ People do not usually react with fear. Surprisingly, there is often a feeling of **euphoria**.

3. ___ You are **on your guard** because of the strangeness of the situation.

4. ___ Differences are likely to seem exciting rather than **threatening**.

5. ___ They might never **recapture** the honeymoon period.

6. ___ Many societies have recent **immigrants**, sometimes in large numbers.

7. ___ Cultural differences can . . . lead to **tense** relationships.

8. ___ They can lead to tense relationships between different **ethnic** groups.

9. ___ Different cultures have to live in close **contact** with each other.

B Work with your partner. Match the vocabulary terms with their definitions. Write the letter of each definition next to the sentence or phrase containing the correct term in Step A. Check your answers in a dictionary if necessary.

a. watching for any danger

b. connection; association

c. get back

d. make a picture of

e. cultural or racial

f. stressful; not calm

g. dangerous

h. intense happiness

i. people who go to live in another country

2 Using a lecturer's diagrams and charts

> Lecturers often use diagrams or charts during a lecture. You can add extra information from the lecture to the diagram or chart as the lecturer speaks.

A Look at a diagram depicting the information Professor Zatz mentioned in Part 2 of the lecture. This diagram represents the "wave" that shows the different stages of culture shock. Notice that the lecturer numbered the stages 1, 2, and 3.

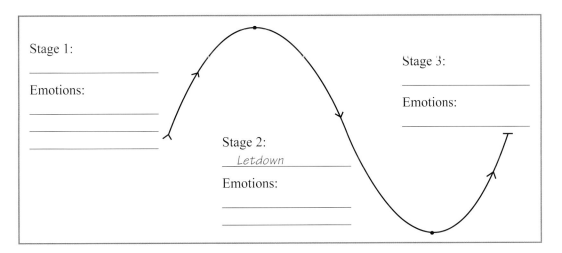

 B As you watch or listen to Part 2 of the lecture, take notes on your own paper. Then use your notes to fill in the diagram with the names of the different stages of culture shock (in the left column) and the different emotions for each stage (in the right column).

Stages of culture shock

Letdown (becoming disappointed because something is not as good as you expected)

Honeymoon (feeling wonderful, like people who take a "honeymoon" trip after they get married)

Resignation (becoming accustomed to a new situation, even if it is difficult)

Emotions of culture shock

adjustment

loneliness

euphoria

excitement

confusion

enthusiasm

C Compare your diagram with a partner.

D Practice giving an oral summary of the three stages of culture shock with your partner.

Sharing your opinion Ⓢ

A Work in a small group. Read the list of behaviors below. Discuss whether these behaviors are acceptable in your community. Why or why not?

1. Kissing your friends two or three times on alternating cheeks when you greet them
2. Holding hands with a person of the same sex when you walk in the street
3. Eating or drinking in the street
4. Pointing at someone with your forefinger
5. Crossing your legs in public

B Work with a partner and look at the pairs of pictures. In your own words, explain why some people might choose one word or the other to describe each picture. Which word would you use for each picture? Why?

work or play?

pleasure or pain?

relaxing or risky?

Unit 1 Academic Vocabulary Review

This section reviews the vocabulary from Chapters 1 and 2. Some of the words that you needed to learn to understand the content of this unit are specific to its topics. Other words are more general. They appear across different academic fields and are extremely useful for all students to know. For a complete list of all the Academic Word List words in this book, see the Appendix on pages 181–182.

A Read the sentences and fill in the blanks with a form of the word.

1. **acquire (v), acquired (adj):**
   We know that children _____ some behavior from their family members. Honesty and discipline, for example, are _____ values.

2. **alternative (adj), alternatively (adv):**
   Single-gender education and coeducation are two _____ models of education. _____ , children may even do *homeschooling*.

3. **benefits (n), beneficial (adj):**
   Families provide many _____ to their members. For example, eating with other members of the family is very _____ for children.

4. **clarify (v), clarified (v), clarification (n):**
   When I was in my early twenties, my father _____ my problems with me. This _____ was very helpful. Families often help children _____ their goals.

5. **concentrate (v), concentration (n):**
   My son's teacher says if he develops his _____ , he will do much better in school. I always tell him to _____ on what he's doing, too.

6. **conflict (n), conflicting (adj):**
   When there is a _____ between children and their parents, most experts say that the two parents should not give _____ opinions. That does not help the situation.

7. **conform (v), conforming (n):** _____ to group behavior is not always a good idea. It's important to use your own judgment, even when there is pressure to _____ .

8. **consequence (n), consequently (adv):**
   People are influenced by others around them. As a _____ , they tend to follow the behavior of the group. _____ , when in a new culture, they often feel like "a fish out of water."

9. **controversy (n), controversial (adj):**
   There is always a lot of _____ about the best way to bring up children. Education, teaching values, and dealing with peer pressure are all _____ topics.

10. **cooperates (v), cooperation (n), cooperative (adj):**
    My daughter _____ well with her peers and her siblings. Being _____ is one of the most important things I've tried to teach her. _____ is a key to success.

11. distinctions (n), distinct (adj):

Every country has _____ customs, values, and beliefs, but sometimes the _____ between them are small.

12. emphasized (v), emphatic (adj):

The lecturer was very _____ when he spoke about cultural differences. I was surprised that he _____ them so much.

13. generation (n), generational (adj):

There are _____ differences, but I think that everyone is affected by his or her peers. In my opinion, the older _____ is also affected by peer pressure.

14. interact (v), interactive (adj):

My friend's daughter likes playing _____ computer games, but I think she should _____ more with other children.

15. react (v), reaction (n):

Why were you surprised when the lecturer mentioned culture shock? I never saw you _____ that way before! I was actually shocked when I saw your _____ .

B Use the academic vocabulary from A above to answer the following questions in pairs or as a class.

Families

1. How and why are families changing?

2. What are some cultural differences related to marriage?

3. What important functions do families play?

Ways of socializing children

4. What are some common ways that parents use to teach children?

5. What are some examples of each method?

6. Why does this issue have so much importance?

Peer pressure

7. What are some examples of peer pressure among adolescents, and how can parents approach it?

8. How can group pressure vary from one community to another?

9. What are some common expressions that relate to groups and individuals?

Culture shock

10. What is culture shock, and why does it occur?

11. What are the stages of culture shock?

12. Why is it important to learn about cultural differences?

Oral Presentation

In academic courses, you will sometimes give oral presentations to a small group about a topic you have researched. Here are some guidelines to keep in mind.

BEFORE THE PRESENTATION

1 Choose a topic

There have been many experiments on group dynamics. Choose one of the following topics that you think will be of interest to your classmates.

1. The **Asch conformity experiments**, in which participants were asked to look at some lines
2. The **Milgram experiment** on people's response to authority figures
3. The phenomenon known as "**six degrees of separation**," which examines social networks
4. The **Robbers Cave experiment,** which studied ways to promote understanding between groups

The ripple effect in water.

5. The **ripple effect**, the **domino effect**, and the **butterfly effect**. These expressions are often used to discuss trends and group behavior.

2 Organize your presentation

1. Research your topic in a library or online. Check at least three different Web sites or texts. Be prepared to answer the following questions:
   - When did the experiment take place?
   - Who was involved?
   - What did the researcher(s) do?
   - What did the study show?
2. Plan what you want to say, but do not write it out and memorize it. Instead, make notes on index cards. Plan to speak for no more than 5 minutes.
3. Organize your notes carefully so that you present your ideas clearly. Introduce your topic as soon as you begin speaking.

Example:

I'm going to tell you about . . . First, I'll give you some details about the experiment: who was involved, where it took place. I'll tell you what the researchers did. Then I'll explain what the study showed. OK, so the experiment was called . . .

4. Consider preparing a visual aid, such as a photograph or chart, to help bring your presentation alive.

DURING THE PRESENTATION

1. Speak as clearly as possible. Remember that you are presenting information that other people probably do not know.
2. Take time to define new words, write proper names on the board, and frequently ask your audience if they understand you or have questions.
3. Consider making a handout with key dates or names. This might make it easier for your audience to follow your presentation.

AFTER THE PRESENTATION

Checking for comprehension

Ask your classmates if they have any questions or comments. Be prepared to give more details on any part of your presentation. Here are some expressions you can use:

Do you have any questions about my presentation?
Can I explain anything in more detail?
Did you understand everything I said?
What do you think about . . . ?
Do you have any comments?

Unit 2
Gender in Society

In this unit, you will hear people talk about gender roles – the way boys and girls are expected to behave. In Chapter 3, you will hear interviews with parents about how they are bringing up their children, and listen to a panel of young adults discuss their own upbringing. You will also listen to a lecture on single-gender education. In Chapter 4, you will hear interviews about gender equality at home and at work. You will listen to a lecturer discuss language use, and the choices people need to make to avoid sexism in language.

Contents

In Unit 2, you will listen to and speak about the following topics.

Chapter 3 Gender Roles	Chapter 4 Gender Issues Today
Interview 1 Bringing Up Children	**Interview 1** Gender Discrimination in the Workplace
Interview 2 Growing Up as a Boy or Girl	**Interview 2** Gender Inequality at Home and in the Workplace
Lecture The Benefits of Single-Gender Education for Girls	**Lecture** Gender and Language

Skills

In Unit 2, you will practice the following skills.

 Listening Skills

Listening for opinions
Drawing inferences
Listening for specific information
Listening for tone of voice

 Speaking Skills

Personalizing the topic
Answering multiple-choice questions
Sharing your opinion
Conducting and discussing a class experiment
Sharing your point of view
Thinking critically about the topic
Examining graphics
Answering true/false questions
Conducting an interview and discussing your findings
Applying what you have learned

 Vocabulary Skills

Reading and thinking about the topic
Personalizing the topic
Building background knowledge on the topic
Examining vocabulary in context
Guessing vocabulary from context

 Note Taking Skills

Using symbols and abbreviations
Using your notes to make an outline
Using telegraphic language

Learning Outcomes

Prepare and **deliver** an oral presentation to demonstrate and support a particular point of view on a topic

Chapter 3
Gender Roles

Look at the picture of a boy and girl and answer the questions with a partner.

1. What are the children doing in this picture?

2. Do you think these children are typical? Do you find their behavior surprising?

1 Getting Started

In this section, you are going to consider the concept of gender and discuss how children learn gender roles. You will also listen to fairy tales that children often learn when they are young, and think about how these stories depict boys and girls in traditional gender roles.

1 Reading and thinking about the topic

A Read the following passage.

Biology determines what *sex* we are at birth – that is, whether we are male or female. However, society and culture determine the *gender roles* we learn – that is, the socially learned patterns of behavior that distinguish boys from girls and men from women.

Some of our behavior may be *innate*, meaning that we are born with it. However, children also learn gender roles through the process of socialization. They learn what society considers masculine and feminine as they grow up and interact with other people. Families, schools, and the media all communicate descriptions of acceptable behavior by men and women. Whether behavior is inherited (innate) or learned (acquired) is often called the "nature/nurture" debate.

However, describing "typical" masculine or feminine behavior is dramatically more complex now than it was in the past. Nowadays, in many countries, boys and girls have more freedom to explore their individuality and less pressure to conform to traditional gender roles.

B Answer the following questions according to the information in the passage.

1. What are gender roles, and how do we learn about them?

2. What is the "nature/nurture" debate?

3. How are gender roles different today?

2 Personalizing the topic Ⓥ Ⓢ

A Read the following list of personality traits. Match the trait with the correct description from the list below and copy the description. Then decide whether you believe these traits are mostly innate (characteristics you are born with) or mostly acquired (learned). Check (✓) the appropriate box. Then compare your answers with a partner.

Trait	Description	Mostly innate	Mostly acquired
1. Athletic ___		☐	☐
2. Brave ___		☐	☐
3. Competitive ___		☐	☐
4. Cooperative ___		☐	☐
5. Independent ___		☐	☐
6. Mischievous ___		☐	☐
7. Passive ___		☐	☐
8. Strong-willed ___		☐	☐
9. Timid ___		☐	☐

a. wants to be more successful than others
b. is good at sports
c. can make decisions alone
d. is not afraid of doing things
e. does what he or she wants to do
f. prefers to be led by others
g. is afraid to talk to others; is shy
h. works well with other people
i. behaves badly

B Now work as a group. Look at the list of traits below and write a short description for each one, checking the dictionary if you need to. Do you think these traits are mostly innate or mostly acquired?

adventurous	cowardly	helpful	nice	sensitive	thoughtful
aggressive	gentle	kind	responsible	sweet	vulnerable

3 Building background knowledge on the topic Ⓥ Ⓢ Ⓛ

A Work in a small group. Look at the pictures below. These pictures illustrate three popular fairy tales – traditional stories handed down from generation to generation – which are often read to children. Read the summaries of the stories and write the personality traits that describe the male and/or female characters in each story. Use traits from "Personalizing the Topic" or your own ideas.

Fairy tale	Summary	Personality traits
1. Jack and the Beanstalk	Jack uses all his family's money to buy some magic beans. His mother is very angry with him because she does not believe the beans are special, and she throws them out the window. When the beans grow, the beanstalk is very tall. Jack climbs the beanstalk and finds the angry giant who stole his family's fortune. Jack kills the giant and gets all the money.	Jack:
2. The Ugly Duckling	A mother duck has seven eggs. When they hatch, six of them are beautiful, but one looks ugly. None of the other ducklings want to be with him, and he is depressed and lonely. He runs away and hides all through the winter in a farmer's house. But something magical happens. In the spring, he sees himself reflected in the water. He is not a duck, but a handsome swan.	Duck:
3. Little Red Riding Hood	Little Red Riding Hood crosses the forest to visit her sick grandmother. On the way, she meets a wolf. The wolf eats her grandmother and then he eats her, too. Luckily, a woodsman kills the wolf and rescues them both.	Little Red Riding Hood: Wolf: Woodsman:

◀)) **B** Now listen to people discussing the fairy tales. In the chart below, write the personality traits they mention and note their opinion.

Fairy tale	Personality traits		Speaker's opinion
	Girls	Boys	
1. Jack and the Beanstalk			
2. The Ugly Duckling			
3. Little Red Riding Hood			

C Share your answers with your group. Discuss how these fairy tales characterize girls and boys. Do you think that fairy tales give good messages to children? Why or why not? Do you think the stories contain stereotypes (oversimplified ideas) about boys and girls? Do you know of any similar stories?

2 Real-Life Voices

In this section, you will hear several people discuss the ways that boys and girls are raised. First, two parents, Andrew and Linda, talk about how they have tried to bring up their children. Then four young people compare the way their parents brought them up.

BEFORE THE INTERVIEWS

Personalizing the topic ⓢ

A In your community, what kind of behavior do parents expect from young girls and boys (under the age of 10)? For each behavior, write *Boys, Girls, Both,* or *Neither.*

TOYS: Who do parents expect to play with . . .

_____ balls?

_____ dolls?

_____ trains and trucks?

_____ paints?

_____ building sets?

_____ other (you choose a toy)? _____

GAMES: Who do parents expect to . . .

_____ play "house" (pretend to do chores)?

_____ play "mommies/daddies" (take care of children)?

_____ play sports?

_____ dress up in costumes?

_____ play musical instruments?

_____ other (you choose a game)? _____

CLOTHES: Who do parents expect to wear . . .

_____ pink clothes?

_____ blue clothes?

_____ pants?

_____ shorts?

_____ jewelry?

_____ other (you choose an item of clothing)? _____

B Older children and teenagers usually have privileges and responsibilities at home (things they are allowed and expected to do). Think about the way you and your friends were treated. For each item, write *Boys, Girls, Both,* or *Neither.*

PRIVILEGES: Who was allowed to . . .

_____ go out after dark?

_____ go out alone?

_____ travel abroad or to another town?

_____ take on a part-time job?

_____ other (you choose a privilege)? _____

RESPONSIBILITIES: Who was asked to . . .

_____ take out garbage?

_____ wash dishes?

_____ clean the house?

_____ cook meals?

_____ repair household items?

_____ other (you choose a responsibility)? _____

C Share your answers to Steps A and B with a partner. Which answers were the same and which were different?

INTERVIEW 1   Bringing Up Children

1 Examining vocabulary in context Ⓥ

Here are some words and phrases from the interview with Andrew and Linda, printed in **bold** and given in the context in which you will hear them. They are followed by definitions.

Do you think parents **raise** boys and girls differently?: *bring up*

There was one **stage** when she would only wear pink: *period of time*

We had to take both of them to the doctor's for a **shot**: *vaccination*

I know they are **exposed to** stereotypes: *made to experience*

The most **critical issue** for me was . . . : *important problem*

They're expected to **excel** in sports: *do extremely well*

There's a major **bonding** that goes on: *feeling of closeness and friendship*

They **tease** each other very **harshly**: *make fun of / in a rough way*

2 Answering multiple-choice questions Ⓢ Ⓛ

> When answering multiple-choice questions, read the directions carefully before you begin. Do you have to choose one answer or two? Do you need to choose the correct answer or the incorrect answer?

A In this interview, Andrew and Linda talk about their goals for their children. Before you listen, read the items and possible answer choices below. For each item, two answers are incorrect and one is correct.

1. Andrew and his wife wanted to treat their children
   a. differently, because one was a boy and one was a girl.
   b. similarly, but making sure they were exposed to gender roles.
   c. the same, so that they would have the same opportunities and experiences.

2. When he was small, Andrew's son enjoyed all of the following, except
   a. getting dirty.
   b. sitting quietly.
   c. getting wet.

3. How was Andrew's daughter different from his son?
   a. She was less typical.
   b. She was more cowardly.
   c. She was more patient.

4. Linda wants her son to be
   a. proud of himself.
   b. good to his parents.
   c. sensitive.

5. Boys are NOT expected to
   a. be tougher.
   b. be better at sports.
   c. form groups easily.

6. Men use sports as
   a. the basis for social relationships.
   b. something to complain about.
   c. a way to relate to women.

7. Many people say that boys are closed emotionally. Linda thinks that boys
   a. are very closed emotionally.
   b. share a lot of their intimate feelings with other boys.
   c. are more open than they used to be in the past.

8. Among the things boys fear, Linda does NOT mention
   a. not being tall enough.
   b. not being accepted.
   c. not being intelligent enough.

🔊 **B** Now listen to what Andrew and Linda say and circle your answers.

C Compare your answers with a partner.

1 Examining vocabulary in context ⓥ

Here are some words and phrases from the interviews with Joy, Sharon, David, and Peter, printed in bold and given in the context in which you will hear them. They are followed by definitions.

Tell me how many **siblings** you had: *brothers and sisters*

There didn't seem to be any **curfew**: *deadline for returning home*

My parents didn't **shelter** me: *protect, sometimes too much*

That was very **supportive** of him: *emotionally encouraging*

I think she really **resented** it: *felt unhappy and angry*

No questions asked: *without raising any objections*

They were just trying to **watch out for** her: *take care of, protect from danger*

2 Listening for specific information ⓛ ⓝ ⓢ

A In these interviews, four people talk about their families. Listen to the interview and take notes on what they say.

	How many siblings does the person have?	Were the children raised the same, or differently?	Examples
Joy			
Sharon			
David			
Peter			

B Compare your answers with a partner and then discuss any differences as a class.

3 Listening for opinions ⓛ ⓢ

🔊 **A** Listen to excerpts of Andrew and Linda discussing their children. For each excerpt, choose the tone that best describes their reaction and place a check (✓).

Excerpt	Amused	Serious	Certain
1	☐	☐	☐
2	☐	☐	☐
3	☐	☐	☐

🔊 **B** Listen to excerpts from the other interviewees. How strongly do the interviewees express their opinions? Check (✓) the correct column.

Excerpt	Not very strongly	Quite strongly	Extremely strongly
4	☐	☐	☐
5	☐	☐	☐
6	☐	☐	☐
7	☐	☐	☐

C Compare your answers with your classmates.

AFTER THE INTERVIEWS

1 Drawing inferences ⓛ ⓢ

Drawing inferences means understanding things that are not directly stated by a speaker. When you listen to people speak, you should not only think about what they tell you directly, but you should also be aware of what they communicate indirectly. Drawing inferences is a critical aspect of listening.

🔊 **A** Listen to the interviews again. For each of the following statements, decide whether you think it correctly reflects what Andrew, Linda, or the panelists inferred in their interviews. Write *T* next to the statement if you think it is true or *F* if you think it is false.

1. Andrew probably thinks that
_____ **a.** parents want their daughters to stay closer to them than their sons.
_____ **b.** parents love their sons and daughters in different ways.

2. Linda probably thinks that
_____ **a.** it isn't easy for girls to make friends if they aren't good at sports.
_____ **b.** boys today communicate with each other better than they did in the past.

3. Joy probably thinks that

___ **a.** she was treated differently than her brother because she was a girl.

___ **b.** parents should raise their children the same, whether they are boys or girls.

4. Sharon probably thinks that

___ **a.** she might have had a different experience if she had many siblings.

___ **b.** her grandmother is old-fashioned.

5. David probably thinks that

___ **a.** girls need more protection than boys.

___ **b.** children of both sexes should have exciting experiences.

6. Peter probably thinks that

___ **a.** nature is just as important as nurture.

___ **b.** all boys should play sports.

B Work with a partner. Check to see if you drew the same inferences. Explain why you thought each answer was true or false. You may disagree about your answers.

2 Sharing your opinion ⑤

A Today boys and girls have many choices about the way they should behave and think. Look at the pictures below and discuss them with a partner. How do you think the interviewees would react to these scenes? What would they say? What is your own reaction to these scenes?

B Many of today's gender roles were unthinkable in our parents' or grandparents' generations. What do you think men and women might do in the future that they don't do now?

3 In Your Own Voice

In this section, you will conduct some research on the way society expects men and women to behave. You will observe groups of men and women and discuss what you see with other students. You will also practice using language to describe an experiment.

Conducting and discussing a class experiment

> Academic lecturers and textbooks often refer to research conducted by experts. It is interesting to try to copy the experts' research experiments on a smaller scale. Doing your own experiments will give you an idea of some of the steps involved in doing more extensive research. It can also provide interesting information and lead to unexpected findings.

A Read some background information.

Many researchers have conducted experiments on gender. Some experiments have involved observing the speech and behavior of thousands of men and women. These experiments have concluded that most men and women obey the "rules" and act the way that society expects them to act.

For example, Robin Tolmach Lakoff discovered that women and men speak in different ways. Women tend to be very polite and apologize more frequently than men do. Deborah Tannen also found that there are differences between the way men and women communicate. For example, men often exchange information, but women tend to discuss their emotions. Because of these differences, men and women often misunderstand each other. Joyce McCarl Nielsen et al., discovered that men and women not only speak differently but also behave differently, acting in ways that seem common for their gender. They made a list of the ways men and women behave in public and discovered that people usually adopt accepted behavior.

B Prepare your own experiment. Look at the list of behaviors below. With a partner, decide if each behavior is commonly associated with men or women, and write *M* (male) or *F* (female).

___ Speaking loudly

___ Talking about feelings

___ Asking a lot of questions

___ Using aggressive body language

___ Talking about cars

___ Talking about sports like baseball, boxing, or football

___ Whispering quietly to another person

___ Playing with hair

___ Wearing perfume

___ Knitting or sewing

___ Painting fingernails or toenails

___ Reading a romance novel

___ Carrying a handbag

___ Opening a door for a member of the opposite sex

___ Crying in public

Other (your own example) _____

C Divide into pairs and conduct your observations out of class. Go to a place where you can watch the behavior of three or four groups of people. Make notes on what you see, using the directions below as a guide. Be very respectful and try not to stare.

1. Describe the people you observed. Give their age, gender, and any other important information.

2. Describe the way the people are speaking. Are they speaking in a way that seems typical for their gender?

3. Describe the way the people are acting. Are they acting in a way that seems typical for their gender?

Useful language for description	
When you describe a person or event, this language can help you:	
1. Many *adjectives* to make your description vivid	*They were young, loud, and energetic.*
2. A *linking verb* with an adjective	*She looked interested. / He seemed excited.*
3. The *past continuous* to describe people's behavior	*She was speaking on her cell phone. / He was wearing aftershave.*

D Describe your findings to other groups.

1. Description of the activity	Examples
Describe where you went. For example, were you inside or outside? How many people were around?	*We went to the mall. We were at the food court at lunchtime, so there were lots of people around.*
2. Results of your observations	
Talk about what happened. What typical male/female behavior did you see? Did you see anything that surprised you?	*We watched a table of women who were in their thirties and forties. They were laughing a lot and touching each other on the arms and shoulders. That surprised me. In my culture, women don't touch each other so much.*
3. What you learned	
How did you feel about doing the experiment? Do you think it is helpful or unhelpful to study common male and female behavior? What are the difficulties involved?	*At first, I felt a little uncomfortable, but no one paid any attention to us, so that was OK. I think it's interesting to study male and female behavior. We could see that there were a lot of differences. I wanted to be closer to hear what they were saying.*

4 Academic Listening and Note Taking

In this section, you will listen and take notes on a two-part lecture given by Dr. Mary Frosch, a teacher at an all-girls' school. The title of the lecture is "The Benefits of Single-Gender Education for Girls." Dr. Frosch will explain why girls seem to learn better when boys are not around.

BEFORE THE LECTURE

1 Building background knowledge on the topic ⓥ ⓢ

A Read the following report about research done in coeducational classrooms.

Studies carried out in coeducational schools show that when boys and girls are in the same classroom, teachers tend to interact with them differently. To begin with, boys get more attention from their teachers. This could be because, in general, boys are more aggressive. One study reported that boys are eight times more likely than girls to call out answers in class.

In addition, some teachers give boys more demanding academic challenges than girls. Boys are expected to be problem solvers, to think for themselves, and to explain their answers. In contrast, girls are usually encouraged to be quiet and well behaved. They are only corrected if they make mistakes. Teachers rarely ask them follow-up questions, and they give them less attention than the boys.

One alternative to coeducation is to separate girls and boys into different classrooms or even different schools. This method is called "single-sex education" or "single-gender education." Some parents and teachers prefer this alternative, but others think that coeducational schools are better.

B Answer the following questions with a partner.

1. What does the term *coeducational* mean? Check a dictionary if necessary.

2. According to the passage, what are the differences between the ways girls and boys are treated in coeducational classes?

3. What do you think? Do you agree that teachers treat boys and girls differently?

C Compare your ideas with your classmates.

2 Sharing your point of view ⓢ ⓝ

A Work in a small group and fill in the chart below with your ideas.

	Single-gender schools	Coed schools
Benefits		
Disadvantages		

B Review your ideas with the class. Then decide whether you are in favor of single-gender education, or against it.

3 Using symbols and abbreviations ⓃⓁⓈ

When you are taking notes during a lecture, you have to write down a lot of information very quickly. Instead of writing out each word separately, you should develop the habit of using symbols and abbreviations. You may want to change some of the symbols and abbreviations below to ones that are easier for you to remember and use. You will probably also want to invent some of your own, depending on the content of the lecture you are attending. When you invent symbols and abbreviations, it is important to review your notes as soon as possible after the lecture while their meanings are still fresh in your mind.

Symbols

Here are some symbols that are commonly used in English. Many of them come from the field of mathematics.

& (and)	= (is the same as, means, equals)
. . . (and so on, etc.)	≠ (is different from, doesn't mean)
@ (at)	< (is less than)
∴ (therefore)	> (is more than)
+ (plus, in addition to)	" (ditto, as said before, similarly)
# (number)	→ (causes, leads to, results in)
$ (dollars)	% (percent)

Abbreviations

In addition to using symbols, good note takers abbreviate long words or words that are frequently used. Here are a few standard abbreviations that are commonly used in English. Notice that some are based on Latin words.

Ex. or e.g. (for example; "e.g." is from the Latin *exempli gratia*)
w/ (with)
etc. (and other similar things, from the Latin *et cetera*)
a.m. (before noon, from the Latin *ante meridiem*)
p.m. (after noon, from the Latin *post meridiem*)
gov't (government)
ed. (education)
Prof. (professor)
Dr. (doctor)
usu. (usually)

> **Pro** and **Con**
>
> pro   (for, a Latin prefix meaning "in favor of")
> con (against, an abbreviation of the Latin *contra*)
>
> When taking notes, these two words are useful. Many texts and lecturers talk about arguments for and against something, or the advantages and disadvantages of something. In such cases, it is easy to simply use the heading *pro* for arguments in favor of something or its advantages, and the heading *con* for arguments against something or its disadvantages. (The terms may be used in the plural as well: *pros* and *cons*.) It is also common for people to use these terms in conversation.

A Study the symbols and abbreviations in the column on the left. Match them with their definitions in the column on the right. You might want to use some of these symbols and abbreviations in your notes for the lecture in this chapter.

1. ♂	**a.** ____ single-sex education
2. ♀	**b.** ____ coeducation, coeducational
3. ed	**c.** ____ boy
4. ben(s)	**d.** ____ different
5. s-s ed	**e.** ____ against, disadvantage
6. →	**f.** ____ opportunities
7. pro	**g.** ____ recommend
8. opps	**h.** ____ and
9. . . .	**i.** ____ benefits
10. coed	**j.** ____ girl
11. diff	**k.** ____ for, in favor of
12. rec	**l.** ____ education, educational
13. &	**m.** ____ causes, leads to, results in
14. con	**n.** ____ and so on, etc.

B Compare your answers with a partner.

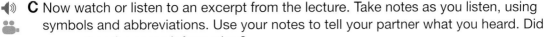

C Now watch or listen to an excerpt from the lecture. Take notes as you listen, using symbols and abbreviations. Use your notes to tell your partner what you heard. Did you gather the same information?

LECTURE PART 1   Pros and Cons of Single-Gender Education for Girls

1 Guessing vocabulary from context Ⓥ

A The following conversation contains important vocabulary from Part 1 of the lecture. Work with a partner and read the conversation aloud. Using the context and your knowledge of related words, take turns guessing the meanings of the words in **bold**.

Andrea: My daughter's about to go to middle school, and my friends were telling me that they send their children to single-gender schools because of all the benefits.

Melanie: Really? I (1) **am not aware of** any reason why they should put boys and girls in separate classrooms.

Andrea: Well, there are lots of reasons. To begin with, boys and girls learn differently. Research has shown that girls get distracted by noise, so it is much (2) **fairer** to allow them to study in a quiet environment.

Melanie: That seems kind of (3) **artificial** to me. Aren't they (4) **missing out on** the opportunity to (5) **interact** with boys?

Andrea: Well, she'll still get to see boys outside of school. But right now, she's kind of shy, so this will help her develop her (6) **self-confidence**.

Melanie: Aren't there any (7) **drawbacks**?

Andrea: Well, single-gender schools are supposed to be pretty (8) **competitive**.

Melanie: That's OK. A little bit of competition won't hurt her. And I'm sure someone will help her (9) **adjust**, right?

Andrea: Yes, I think so.

B Work with your partner. Match the vocabulary items from Step A with their definitions. Write the number on the line.

a. ___ disadvantages

b. ___ do not know about

c. ___ feeling that you can manage any situation

d. ___ full of competition

e. ___ more just, appropriate

f. ___ losing

g. ___ talk to, spend time with

h ___ get used to something

i. ___ unnatural

2 Using symbols and abbreviations Ⓝ Ⓛ

A Look at these notes on Part 1 of the lecture. Think about what kind of information might belong in the blanks. Notice that these notes are formatted in columns. The cons are in the first (left) column because these are the first aspects of the topic that Dr. Frosch presents. The pros are in the second (right) column. Putting your notes in columns labeled "Pros" and "Cons" is often an effective way to organize notes.

Dr. Mary Frosch: The Benefits of Single-Sex Education for Girls
Part 1: Disadvantages and Advantages of Single-Sex Education for Girls
Cons

Pros (Dr. F. is pro s-s ed)

• Old-fashioned –
  ed. opps. diff. for ♂ & ♀

• _____

  _____   • _____

                                                      _____

  _____   • _____

  • _____

    _____   _____

  _____

B Now watch or listen to Part 1 of the lecture. Take notes on your own paper. Remember to use symbols and abbreviations.

C Use your own notes to complete the notes in Step A.

D Compare your completed notes for Step A with a partner.

1 Guessing vocabulary from context Ⓥ Ⓢ

A Read the discussion between two middle school teachers and fill in the blanks with the words below.

Alison (an experienced teacher): Hi, Jeff. How are things going in your classes?

Jeff (a new teacher): Excuse me?

Alison: Oh, I was asking how things were going.

Jeff: I'm sorry. There was a lot of noise in the hallway. There are so many (1) _____ in school, right? But yes, things are going well. I'm (2) _____ that they'll get even better after a few weeks.

Alison: What kind of activities have you been doing in class?

Jeff: Well, I think it is important for students to learn to work together, so I've been giving the kids a lot of (3) _____ activities. And they're adolescents, so you know, I want them to be proud of what they do and develop their (4) _____ .

Alison: Have you had any problems with discipline?

Jeff: Oh, no. The kids seem to (5) _____ each other a lot. I would say that (6) _____ , the girls seem to be more mature than the boys – and I think they are better at (7) _____ thinking. The boys prefer to solve problems, and they need to be very active in class.

Alison: Don't you think that's a stereotype?

Jeff: Well, maybe it is. I don't know – I try to treat my students the same. And I encourage all of them to ask questions if they need (8) _____ about a topic we're studying.

Alison: It sounds as if you are doing really well. I wish you the best of luck!

Jeff: Thank you so much for your (9) _____ , Alison. I really appreciate it.

abstract	confident	respect
clarification	distractions	self-esteem
collaborative	emotionally	support

B Work with a partner and compare your answers. Then read the conversation aloud.

2 Using your notes to make an outline ⓝ ⓛ

Outlining is an essential study skill. It means organizing the notes you have taken on a lecture (or part of a lecture) to a few key points. A good outline shows that you have understood what the lecture is about and what the most important points are. It is a helpful record for you to review when you are studying for a test.

During the lecture, take notes in whatever way works best for you. After the lecture, revise your notes as soon as possible. Make sure they are in a clear format and add any missing information. Then use your notes to help you construct an outline. Reread your notes and select the most important points that the lecturer made. Make an outline in which you explain the main points in your own words.

A Watch or listen to Part 2 of the lecture and take notes in whatever way works best for you. Remember to use symbols and abbreviations.

B Organize your notes in an appropriate format. Do you want to put your notes into columns as you did for Part 1? Do you think an outline form would be better? Or do you have another way that you would like to organize your notes?

C The following is an outline of Part 2 of the lecture. Use your notes to complete the outline. You may need to put more than one word in some blanks. Then compare outlines with your partner. Do you have similar answers?

The Benefits of Single-Gender Education for Girls
Part 2: Two Main Benefits of All-Girls' Schools
Dr. Mary Frosch

Single-sex education has 2 main _____ for girls:
    I. recognizes girls' _____
       A. girls can concentrate on _____
       B. girls can _____ for long periods
       C. girls enjoy _____, so they like to work _____
       D. girls are _____ and _____

    II. allows girls to become _____
       A. ask for _____ if they need it
       B. if boys are around, _____

    III. Dr. F. admits that:
       A. recently, girls _____
       B. all-girls' schools DO separate the sexes
       C. BUT, she thinks _____

Thinking critically about the topic ⓢ

One way to practice thinking critically about an issue is to argue both in favor of it and against it. After doing this, you may find that you still strongly hold your original opinion, or you may find that you have changed your mind.

A Look at the statements below. Put an *A* in front of each statement that you agree with. Put a *D* in front of each statement that you disagree with.

1. ___ The idea of having separate schools for boys and girls is old-fashioned.
2. ___ Some girls are just as aggressive as boys are.
3. ___ If you put adolescent boys and girls together, they concentrate more on each other than they do on their classes.
4. ___ Girls work together much better if there are no boys around.
5. ___ Boys can get very loud in class, and then they get all the teacher's attention.
6. ___ Boys and girls don't work well together.
7. ___ It is more natural to have coed schools.

B Work in a group of three students. Take turns in the "hot seat." If it is your turn, explain why you agree with one of the statements in Step A. The other two students should strongly disagree with the statement you are defending. Think of as many arguments for and against each statement as possible. Here are some ways to express disagreement or to ask for clarification:

Expressing disagreement	Asking for clarification
I'm not sure if I agree with you because . . .	*Excuse me, are you saying . . . ?*
I'm afraid that I disagree with you because . . .	*I'm sorry, but I don't understand what you mean when you say (that) . . .*
I don't agree with your explanation of . . . because . . .	*Can you explain that again?*
I think that you're wrong because . . .	*Can you give us some more information about . . . ?*
	Why do you think (that) . . . ?

C As a class, discuss whether or not you changed your opinion about any of the statements in Step A as a result of your discussions in Step B.

Chapter 4
Gender Issues Today

Look at the photographs and answer the questions with a partner.

1. How might the man taking care of his young son feel? What are some benefits of taking care of his baby? What difficulties might he face?

2. What are some problems facing the woman at her computer? What do you think she is proud of? What do you think she finds difficult?

1 Getting Started

In this section you are going to discuss changes in traditional gender roles. You will also listen to a conversation about gender stereotypes, which are fixed ideas about what men and women are like.

1 Reading and thinking about the topic

A Read the following passage.

The feminist movement, also called the women's movement, has existed since the eighteenth century. In the early years, it was mainly concerned with voting rights for women. In the twentieth century, it became concerned with gender inequality in the workplace and the home.

In the past hundred years, women across the world have made progress toward gaining equal opportunities in education. More women have also entered the workforce. Both girls and boys are now encouraged to choose careers they are interested in. They no longer feel that they have to choose careers that are "traditional" for their gender. At home, husbands and wives have begun to share household *chores* (everyday tasks) and care of their children.

These changes in gender roles have helped many women advance toward gaining equal rights in many areas of life. However, sociologists agree that the problem of gender inequality is still a serious issue today because not all women have benefited from this progress.

B Answer the following questions according to the information in the passage.

1. When did the women's movement begin?
2. How did people's lives change in the twentieth century, whether they were men or women?
3. What do sociologists believe about gender inequality today?

C Read these questions and share your answers with a partner.

1. Can you give an example from your own experience of inequality between men and women?
2. What are the biggest obstacles affecting men and women today, in your opinion?

2 Examining graphics ⓢ

A Look at the bar graph below that shows the average amount earned by men and women in the United States.

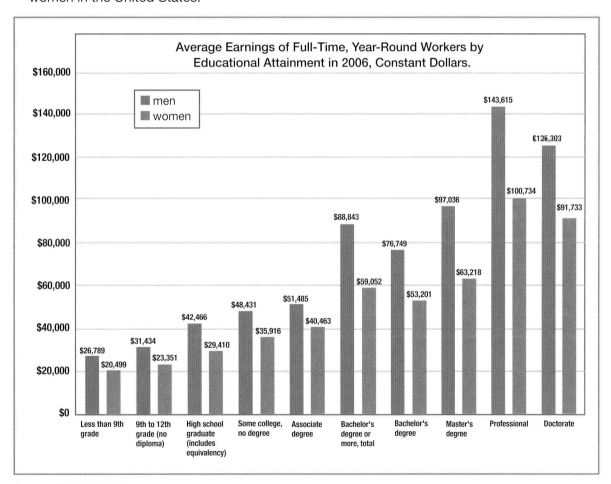

Average Earnings of Full-Time, Year-Round Workers by Educational Attainment in 2006, Constant Dollars.

Source: Statistical Abstract

B Discuss the following questions with a partner.

1. What is the effect of education on men's and women's salaries?

2. In what way have women made progress? What progress do they still need to make?

3. What information in the chart particularly surprises or interests you?

3 Listening for specific information

A Read the beginning of a conversation between Jack and Sheila, a married couple. They are discussing an article Jack read about gender stereotypes.

> **Jack:** Hey, Sheila, I just finished reading an interesting article about gender inequality in the workplace. It's by Natasha Josefowitz.
>
> **Sheila:** What does she say?
>
> **Jack:** Well, she talks about common situations that happen to employees who work in offices. Here are some of them:
>
> The employee is going to get married.
>
> The employee has a family picture on his or her desk.
>
> The employee is talking with a co-worker.
>
> The employee is going to go on a business trip.
>
> Then she says that co-workers react differently depending on whether the employee in the situation is a man or a woman.
>
> **Sheila:** You mean that people react differently if, for example, the person getting married is a man or a woman? Tell me what the article says.
>
> **Jack:** OK. Let me see what I can remember.

B Discuss the following questions with a partner.

How do you think people react differently to the situations Jack mentions if the employee is a man or a woman? Why?

C Listen to what Jack remembers about the situations in the article. Take notes on your own paper.

D Compare your notes for Step C with your partner. Did you understand the same things?

2 Real-Life Voices

In this section, you will hear Belinda, a successful American entertainer and filmmaker, describe her feelings about discrimination against women in the workplace. Then you will hear Farnsworth, a social worker who helps people with emotional problems, give his views on gender discrimination at home and in the workplace.

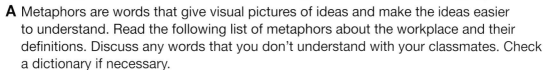

BEFORE THE INTERVIEWS

Building background knowledge on the topic 🅥 🅢

A Metaphors are words that give visual pictures of ideas and make the ideas easier to understand. Read the following list of metaphors about the workplace and their definitions. Discuss any words that you don't understand with your classmates. Check a dictionary if necessary.

1. *Glass ceiling:* The glass ceiling is the invisible barrier that women often "hit" as they try to get promoted to higher positions within a company.

2. *Glass escalator:* The glass escalator is the invisible machine that seems to promote men to higher positions.

3. *Sticky floor:* The sticky floor is the force that seems to hold women back in less important and lower paid positions.

4. *Old boys' club:* This refers to the all-male groups that men form and the connections they make with each other to help themselves gain power and success.

5. *Mommy track:* People often think that working women with children are not serious about their jobs. They say that these women are on the "mommy track." That is, they are not on the road – or "track" – that leads to higher positions.

6. *Level playing field:* The level playing field is like a sports field in which all the players are on the same level and have the same chance to win. Having a level playing field means that no one group has more opportunity to succeed than any other group.

7. *To get a foot in the door:* To take a first step toward getting a job. It refers to the fact that it is difficult for women to enter some professions.

B Match each of the following situations with one of the metaphors in Step A. Write the number on the line.

a. ___ A woman talking to her friend about her boss:
"Since my baby was born, my boss looks at me strangely every time I get sick and take a day off. I'm sure he thinks that I just want to stay home with my baby."

b. ___ A sales manager talking to another sales manager who was just hired:
"Don't worry, Sam. We'll help you with your new position. What about getting together with some of the guys after work tonight?"

c. ___ A company director talking to a personnel manager:
"We need to hire a new office assistant. Be sure to tell the people you interview that all employees are encouraged to apply when higher positions become available."

d. ___ Two employees talking about a third employee:
"He's gone from sales clerk to assistant manager to manager in 18 months. That's a record!"

e. ___ An excerpt from a business report:
"There are about 50 female executive vice presidents in the largest companies, but only two female chief executive officers."

f. ___ A woman talking to her friend:
"Even though I have good skills, everywhere I go, I seem to get offered the lowest paid positions."

g. ___ A woman talking to her husband:
"I'm so excited about my interview next week. I know not many women work in this position, but I've taken the first step by getting the chance to talk to the boss in person."

C Discuss the following questions in a small group.

1. Do you think that the metaphors listed in Step A give an accurate picture of the situations men and women face in the workplace?

2. Can you give any examples of these metaphors from your own experience?

D Look at the cartoon. Do you think most people would agree with its message?

Gender Discrimination in the Workplace

1 Examining vocabulary in context ⓥ

Here are some words and expressions from the interview with Belinda, printed in **bold** and given in the context in which you will hear them. They are followed by definitions.

The first answer is yes – that's my **gut** feeling: *deep and immediate*

That's absolutely **awful**: *terrible, bad*

I have **mixed feelings**: *feelings that are in conflict with each other*

Sometimes I think that I'm just **making excuses for myself**: *finding reasons not to feel bad about myself*

Women **tend to** think of helping . . . others: *usually*

2 Answering multiple-choice questions Ⓢ Ⓝ Ⓛ

A Read the following questions before you listen to the interview. Which answer do you think is probably correct?

1. The interviewer asks Belinda if she has ever been discriminated against because she is a woman. Belinda answers:
a. Yes.
b. No.
c. Yes and no.
d. Not sure.

2. The question that Belinda asks herself is:
a. Should I talk to my boss about getting promoted?
b. Am I as good as the men?
c. Would I be making more progress if I were male?
d. What would my brother do in my position?

3. Belinda's feeling about the current situation in the workplace is that
a. there has been no progress toward gender equality.
b. women should form their own support groups.
c. there is more opportunity for women today than in the past.
d. women will never have gender equality.

4. Belinda thinks that women
a. usually think about themselves more than men do.
b. help themselves and other people, too.
c. work much harder than men.
d. can't make a place for themselves in the business world.

B Now listen to the interview. Take notes on what Belinda says. Use your notes to choose the best response for each question in Step A. Circle one choice for each question.

C Compare your answers with a partner.

INTERVIEW 2 Gender Inequality at Home and in the Workplace

1 Examining vocabulary in context Ⓥ

Here are some words and expressions from the interview with Farnsworth, printed in **bold** and given in the context in which you will hear them. They are followed by definitions.

a **pay disparity**: *difference in pay*

There have been changes . . . , but they've been **relatively modest**: *not very large or important*

Ninety percent of my **colleagues** are women: *co-workers*

both the **CEO** and his boss: *chief executive officer – one of the most important positions in a company*

Men are . . . raised with a sense of **entitlement**: *a feeling that they deserve the best opportunities*

if they are divorced and have **custody**: *legal responsibility for a child*

Women just **assume** that they can do it: *feel that they can do it even though they haven't done it before*

I joined a **playgroup** with my son: *a group of mothers and/or fathers that meets so that their children can play together*

He wasn't *really* an **active parent**: *a parent who is physically involved in caring for his or her children*

2 Answering true/false questions Ⓢ Ⓛ

When answering true/false questions, read all parts of each statement carefully. Some parts of a statement may be true, but if any part of it is false, then the whole statement is false. Pay special attention to statements with negatives in them. These statements are often tricky. Remember that a negative statement that is correct is true.

A Read the following statements before you listen to the interview with Farnsworth.

___ **1.** Farnsworth believes that there is real equality between men and women now.

___ **2.** Women make as much money as men do, so the "pay disparity" that used to exist doesn't exist anymore.

___ **3.** Farnsworth believes that the glass ceiling exists because at his job men hold most of the higher paid positions.

___ **4.** Farnsworth believes that there is much more equality between the sexes at home. Men and women tend to share the housework.

___ **5.** Farnsworth wishes he had been more active in raising his children. He thinks he should have helped out more when they were babies with tasks like giving them a bottle at night and cooking.

___ **6.** Farnsworth says that when divorced men get custody of their children, they often don't feel that they can take good care of the children.

___ **7.** When his son was small, Farnsworth joined a children's playgroup. He was the only man involved in this activity.

🔊 **B** Now listen to the interview. Write *T* (true) or *F* (false) next to each of the statements in Step A.

C Compare answers with a partner. Correct the false statements together.

3 Listening for tone of voice Ⓛ Ⓢ

🔊 **A** Read the following statements. Then listen to the excerpts. Circle the tone that best corresponds to Belinda's and Farnsworth's comments.

1. The interviewer asks if Belinda has ever been discriminated against because she is a woman. Belinda
   a. hesitates.
   b. sounds angry.
   c. acts surprised.

2. Belinda is comparing the situation in the past with the situation today. She sounds
   a. unsure.
   b. emphatic.
   c. frustrated.

3. When she is asked if successful women help other women succeed, Belinda
   a. responds after thinking carefully.
   b. answers immediately.
   c. seems to have no enthusiasm.

4. The interviewer asks Farnsworth about equality today. Farnsworth
   a. is unsure what he thinks.
   b. has strong feelings about the topic.
   c. has to think before responding.

5. Farnsworth discusses his own father. He thinks
   a. his father was actively involved with his children.
   b. his father did not participate in bringing up the children.
   c. his father helped a little, but not a lot.

B Compare your answers with a partner.

AFTER THE INTERVIEWS

1 Thinking critically about the topic Ⓢ Ⓝ

A Belinda and Farnsworth talk about the increase in the number of women who work and the increase in the number of men who want to be active parents. Read the following problem situations. Discuss a possible solution to each problem with a partner, preferably someone of the opposite sex. Make notes about your solutions.

1. A divorced father has custody of three young children. When they get sick and cannot go to school, he has to use his own sick days – days that employees are allowed to take off if they are sick – to stay home from work and take care of them.

   Possible solution: _Employers could allow employees with children a certain number of "sick child days" per year in addition to their own personal sick days._

2. A company often asks its employees to do overtime – that is, work longer than the normal workday. One employee doesn't want to do overtime because she wants to spend her evenings with her children.

   Possible solution: _____

   _____

3. A young father would like to spend time with his newborn baby. He requests a six-month leave of absence without pay. The company tells him that it cannot guarantee that he will get his same job back after the leave.

Possible solution: _____

_____

4. An employee has a new baby. She needs to make more money so that she can afford child care because she and her husband both work.

Possible solution: _____

_____

5. A company offers a woman a promotion, and she must decide whether or not to accept it. Her new job would involve having to fly to other cities once or twice a month, so she would spend more time away from her family.

Possible solution: _____

_____

B Share your solutions with the class. How different are your classmates' solutions?

2 Examining graphics ⑤

A Look at the map below. It shows the "gender gap" in pay around the world.

Salary ratio of women to men

KEY
- >0.7
- 0.6–0.7
- 0.5–0.6
- 0.4–0.5
- <0.4
- No data

Source: www.wikigender.org. Data from UNDF

B Work with a partner. Take turns describing what the map shows about the difference between men's and women's salaries.

C In your opinion, what are some factors that cause women to earn less than men all over the world? Share your ideas with the class.

3 In Your Own Voice

In this section, you will interview a few men and women about the issues that active parents face today. You will begin by gathering some background information on the topic. After your interviews, you will present your findings to the class and give each other feedback on your presentations.

Conducting an interview and discussing your findings Ⓢ Ⓝ Ⓥ

> An interview is a meeting in which someone who wants to learn more about a topic asks questions of another person – usually a person who has personal knowledge of the topic. Conducting interviews can be a useful way for students to increase their knowledge. An interview will be more successful if the interviewer gathers background information about the topic beforehand and uses this information to prepare questions.

A Read the following information about the mommy track and the daddy track.

You have probably heard the expression "mommy track." This refers to the problems that mothers often face as they try to juggle family and work responsibilities. For example, women with children who do not want to work overtime may not get promoted to high positions.

As more and more fathers take an active role in the care of their children, they are finding that they face similar problems. This phenomenon is called the "daddy track." For example, if fathers take some time off work after their children are born – this time off is called *paternity leave* – they might be criticized by their boss or their colleagues and not get promoted.

B Work with a partner and gather background information about the problems that active mothers and fathers face today. You can do this through the resources of a library, such as encyclopedias or other reference books and textbooks, or through an Internet search. Here are some keywords that you could use to get started.

- mommy track/daddy track
- maternity leave/paternity leave
- flexible hours
- dependent children
- promotions
- child care

Here are some examples of the kind of information you might look for.

- percentage of men and women who stay at home with their children while their wives or husbands work
- problems men and women face at home and at work because they want to be active parents
- benefits of spending time with young children
- similarities and differences between women on the mommy track and men on the daddy track

C Plan your interview carefully.

1. Plan the language you will need to use to ask people outside of class to help you conduct your interviews. Here is an example.

My name is . . . and I'm studying gender issues in my class. My teacher has asked me to conduct some surveys outside of class. Would you mind helping me? I will ask you three or four questions and ask for your opinion. I will take notes on what you say and use the information you give me to have a class discussion.

2. Use the information you found in Step B to prepare three to five questions for your interviews. Number your questions. Here are some example questions.

How old are your children? Who stays with them during the day?

How active are you as a mother or father? Can you give an example of the activities you do with your children?

Do you have difficulty juggling your work responsibilities and your family life?

What kinds of difficulties do you face as a working parent?

Is it true that . . . ? (add something you read about in your research)

Do you agree that . . . ? (add something you read about in your research)

D Make a chart on a separate paper in which you can organize your notes.

	Questions asked	Person's responses	Other relevant information
Person #			
Name:			
Age:			
Gender:			
Nationality:			

E Interview at least three people outside of class and take notes on what they say. Try to arrange interviews with working men and women who have children.

F After the interviews, share your experience with your classmates. Tell your partner what you did and what happened. Ask your classmates questions about what they say.

4 Academic Listening and Note Taking

In this section you will hear and take notes on a two-part lecture given by Wendy Gavis, a professor of linguistics. The title of the lecture is "Gender and Language." Professor Gavis will discuss how to avoid sexism in language, and will respond to students' questions.

BEFORE THE LECTURE

1 Building background knowledge on the topic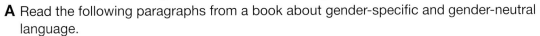

A Read the following paragraphs from a book about gender-specific and gender-neutral language.

When speaking or writing, it is important to avoid using gender-specific terms wherever possible because these terms can show sexism – that is, prejudice and discrimination based on a person's gender. The term *chairman*, for example, is often used to refer to a person who is the leader of a meeting, a committee, or an organization. But chairman implies that the position is always held or can only be held by a man. Instead, a gender-neutral term such as *chair* or *chairperson* can be used. Similarly, a term like *woman doctor* should be avoided since a doctor can be male or female.

In English, it is difficult to be gender-neutral when using pronouns. Grammatically, "a good doctor submits his reports on time" is correct. However, so is "a good secretary types his letters on time" and "a good shopper always does his shopping before the crowds arrive."

B Discuss the following questions with a partner.

1. What is a "gender-specific" term? Can you think of some examples?
2. What is a "gender-neutral" term? Can you think of some examples?
3. Why is it difficult to be gender-neutral when using pronouns in English?
4. What do the pronouns used in the second paragraph of the reading imply about the doctor, the secretary, and the shopper?

2 Using telegraphic language Ⓝ Ⓛ

When you listen to a lecture, it is not possible to write down everything the lecturer says. Good note takers are able to write down the most important information in as few words as possible. Using telegraphic language will help you to do this quickly. Telegraphic language is abbreviated language that reads like newspaper headlines.

When you use telegraphic language, you usually don't include the following:
Articles (*a, an,* and *the*)
The verb *to be* and other linking verbs
Prepositions and pronouns

Look at this example of telegraphic language.

Original sentences
The first topic I will discuss is the large increase in the number of students who attend college today compared with the past. There has been a large increase of both male and female students.

Telegraphic language
Topic 1: Large incr. in # of Ss in college today compared to past – ♂ & ♀.
Notice that the note taker has also used abbreviations and symbols. Using telegraphic language together with symbols and abbreviations will help you to become a good note taker.

A Read the following summaries of different parts of the lecture.

_____ **a.** The topic of today's lecture is sexism in language and how to avoid it.

_____

_____ **b.** There are a great many gender-specific terms. Words like *mailman* or *policeman* are gender-specific because they only refer to men.

_____

_____ **c.** The word *mankind* sounds as if you are only talking about men, but when you say *human beings* or *people*, then you include both men and women.

_____

_____ **d.** The words we use affect how we think. For example, if children grow up hearing *chairman*, they think the title must always refer to a man.

_____

 B Now watch or listen to the four short excerpts and match them with the correct summaries. Write the number of each excerpt on the correct line in Step A.

C On the line following each summary in Step A, rewrite the summary in telegraphic language. Use symbols and abbreviations whenever you can.

1 Guessing vocabulary from context Ⓥ

The following items contain important vocabulary from Part 1 of the lecture. Work with a partner. Using the context and your knowledge of related words, circle the best synonym for the words in bold. Check your answers in a dictionary if necessary.

___ **1.** Everyone should pick up his pen – or **rather**, everyone should pick up her pen.

    a. actually

    b. preferably

    c. alternatively

___ **2.** You **get my point**, right?

    a. understand me

    b. agree with me

    c. aren't sure

___ **3.** I'm going to **specifically** discuss sexism in language.

    a. generally

    b. precisely

    c. lastly

___ **4.** Language **conveys** a lot of messages about gender.

    a. has

    b. communicates

    c. includes

___ **5.** A safe **option** is to use what we call "gender-neutral" terms.

    a. method

    b. probability

    c. choice

___ **6.** Children **internalize** the idea that all leaders are men.

    a. reject

    b. question

    c. get

___ **7.** I'm facing a **dilemma**.

    a. controversial topic

    b. difficult choice

    c. hard fact

___ **8.** **As far as I'm concerned**, that's very important.

    a. in my opinion

    b. I agree with other people

    c. most people say the same as me

2 Using telegraphic language ⓝ ⓛ

A Look at these notes on Part 1 of the lecture. Notice how the note taker uses telegraphic language, symbols, and abbreviations. (Review the list of symbols and abbreviations in "Note Taking: Using Symbols and Abbreviations," page 57 if necessary.) Read the notes and think about what kind of information might belong in the blanks.

Prof. Wendy Gavis: Gender and Language

Pt 1: Gender-specific and gender-neutral language

I. Main idea: _____

II. Gen-spec. lang.

    A. Def: _____

    B. Ex:

           1. mail   <u>man</u>

           2. _____   "

           3. _____   "

III. _____ lang shows

    A. World as is – ♀ can have same jobs as ♂ (Ex: _____ & _____ & _____)

    B. Equality (Ex: _____)

IV. _____

    A. Choices

           1. Everyone pick up <u>his</u> pen.

           2. "   " "___".

           3. _____

    B. Gravis uses _____ – not gram., but solves prob.

    C. _____

B Now watch or listen to Part 1 of the lecture. Take notes on your own paper using telegraphic language. Use symbols and abbreviations wherever you can.

C Use your own notes to complete the notes in Step A.

D Compare the notes you took and your completed notes for Step A with a partner.

1 Guessing vocabulary from context Ⓥ Ⓢ

A The following items contain important vocabulary from Part 2 of the lecture. Work with a partner. Using the context and your knowledge of related words, take turns guessing the meanings of the words in **bold**.

___ **1.** the way the **mass media** treats women

___ **2.** the way they **stereotype** women

___ **3.** The language question is also **on the minds of** international organizations.

___ **4.** The girls just stand **in the background**.

___ **5.** By focusing on the language we use about women, we may be able to change their **expectations**.

___ **6.** Does this **controversy** . . . exist in other languages, too?

___ **7.** It is definitely receiving . . . more attention **worldwide**.

B Work with your partner. Match the vocabulary terms from Step A with their definitions. Write the letter on the line. Check your answers in a dictionary if necessary.

a. channels of communication – such as television, radio, and newspapers – that reach large numbers of people

b. ideas that we have about the way people should behave

c. in a position of less importance

d. everywhere in the world

e. being considered by

f. present a fixed, narrow idea of what they are like

g. debate, dilemma

2 Using telegraphic language Ⓝ Ⓛ Ⓢ

A Read the following questions about gender and language. Think about the kind of information you might hear in response to these questions.

1. There are many very serious gender issues facing society today. How important is the language question?

2. If we change the way we talk about people, does that mean we change the way we think about them?

3. Does gender-specific language occur in other languages besides English? Does the same controversy exist everywhere about using gender-neutral language?

B Now watch or listen to Part 2 of the lecture. Take notes on your own paper using telegraphic language. Use the questions in Step A as a guide to help you listen for the important points.

C Work with a partner. Looking at the telegraphic language you and your partner have used, take turns answering the questions in Step A orally.

Applying what you have learned Ⓢ

> Finding ways to apply what you have learned is a good way to deepen your understanding of new subject matter.

A Look at the cartoon. What is it saying? How does it relate to the lecture?

"Blivens, how would you like to be a member of the old boy's club?"

B Read the following excerpt from a student's essay. Notice how difficult it is for the student to use pronouns and verbs correctly. Rewrite the paragraph using plural nouns and pronouns where appropriate. In this way, you can avoid sexism and also avoid using *he/she, his/her*, or *him/her.* You may also need to change verbs to agree with the subject. Compare your completed paragraph with two other classmates.

It is not easy to have a career if you are a mother or father of a young child. A working parent is responsible to her children in addition to her job. It is really hard to take care of both responsibilities at the same time. However, according to a report I just read, some companies are trying to be more sensitive to the needs of working mothers and fathers. For example, if the employee is late one day, the company should not automatically assume that he/she is acting irresponsibly. If the employee has children, he/she sometimes has a problem getting to work on time. It is better for the company to be flexible because the employee will do his job better if he or she feels supported at work.

Unit 2 Academic Vocabulary Review

This section reviews the topics and vocabulary from Chapters 3 and 4. For a complete list of all the Academic Word List words in this book, see the Appendix on pages 181–182.

A Complete the following sentences with the correct word forms. Note: You will not use all of the word forms given.

1. **accuracy (n), accurate (adj), inaccurate (adj):**
   It is _____ to say that people all behave in the same way. _____ is very important in experiments about people's behavior.

2. **adjust (v), adjusting (v), adjustment (n):**
   Now that he has begun college, he is _____ well to his new environment. The _____ period usually takes about a month.

3. **adult (n), adulthood (n):**
   As adolescents enter the period of _____ , they begin to be more sensitive to gender roles.

4. **availability (n), available (adj), unavailable (adj):**
   The government is working hard to increase the _____ of jobs across the country. Many job opportunities that existed in the past are _____ today.

5. **awareness (n), aware (adj), unaware (adj):**
   My brother was _____ of the obstacles women face in the workplace until he and his wife had a child. I lis new _____ means that he will do anything he can to help his wife succeed in her career.

6. **bond (v), bonding (n):**
   They say that male _____ is very strong. However, I think that women _____ with other women, too.

7. **challenge (v), challenge (n), challenging (adj):**
   Teenagers often _____ their parents' authority. The teenage years can be quite a _____ time.

8. **communicate (v), communication (n):**
   Experts agree that _____ is the key to a successful work environment.

9. **discriminate (v), discrimination (n), discriminatory (adj):**
   Gender _____ is forbidden under the law. However, in practice, many women say people _____ against them at work.

10. **expert (n), expertise (n):**
    If they are allowed to explore many different subjects, children often develop an _____ in something that really interests them.

11. **individual (n), individuality (n), individualistic (adj):**
    My son is a true _____ . He rarely does what others expect. He tends to be very _____ .

12. intelligence (n), intelligent (adj), unintelligent (adj):

Some _____ tests are not good. They ask questions that can be considered sexist, such as questions about cars, sports, or cooking. If children get the questions wrong, they could be considered _____ .

13. similarities (n), similar (adj), similarly (adv):

Both men and women experience _____ challenges. We often talk about the differences between the sexes, but of course there are many _____ , too.

14. tradition (n), traditional (adj), traditionally (adv):

_____ , women have taken more responsibility for housework. Now they are questioning the _____ role of "housewife."

15. visibility (n), invisible (adj):

Many women believe that there are _____ ceilings that stop them from getting promoted.

B With a small group, answer the questions below. In your responses, use some of the vocabulary from A above.

Nature/nurture

1. What is the nature/nurture debate about?

2. What are some common fairy tales, and what do they teach children about gender?

3. What are some stereotypes about boys and girls?

Single-gender education

4. Why do some people think single-sex education is better than coeducation?

5. How might boys and girls learn in different ways?

6. Why is single-gender education such a complex issue?

Gender issues in the workplace

7. What are some common metaphors that people use to discuss gender issues?

8. What does the term *pay disparity* mean?

9. Are women treated equally in the workplace?

Sexism in language

10. How can we avoid using sexist language?

11. What are gender-specific terms and gender-neutral terms?

12. Why is it considered important to avoid using sexist language?

Oral Presentation

You will make a 5-minute presentation to the class in which you present a point of view and explain it using several reasons and examples.

BEFORE THE PRESENTATION

1 Choose a point of view

Read the following statements and decide whether you agree or disagree with them. Then choose one statement to support, or prepare a similar statement of your own.

1. Nature is more important than nurture.
2. Parents should treat their sons and daughters exactly the same.
3. Women face a lot of discrimination, so it is difficult for them to get highly paid jobs.
4. It is just as important for women as it is for men to have a career.
5. Men and women should share equally in making money and doing housework.
6. Both parents should share the responsibility of taking care of their children.
7. There are some professions that can only be practiced by a man or a woman.

2 Organize your presentation

It is very important to organize your presentation well. Like essays, good presentations have an introduction, body, and conclusion.

	Examples
Introduction: Tell your audience a personal story or a shocking statistic to get them interested in what you have to say. Then present your opinion.	*When I was growing up, I always wanted a tool set. My mother and father went right out and bought one for me, even though I was a girl. I think that parents should treat their sons and daughters exactly the same. All children should have the same toys.* or *Do you realize that less than 5 percent of the top companies in my country have a woman as their chief executive officer? I think women face a lot of discrimination at work.*
Body: Try to come up with at least three reasons to support your viewpoint. Link these ideas with transitions, just as you would do in a written assignment. Explain these ideas and then make sure that you provide interesting examples to help you make your point.	*First of all, . . .* *Not only that, but . . .* *Lastly, . . .*
Conclusion: Repeat your main idea. Use different words to communicate your opinion.	*So, let me summarize my ideas.* *As you can see, . . .* *Now you understand that . . .*

1. Use effective body language. Relax, but do not act too informally. Stand up straight, and do not put your hands in your pockets or on your hips. Use your hands to communicate your feelings.

2. Make eye contact. You are trying to explain a point of view that some people may disagree with. If you look people directly in the eye and are sincere, you will have a much stronger presentation.

3. Speak slowly, loudly, and confidently. Remember that your audience does not know what you are going to say. Pause from time to time to make sure that your classmates are following your presentation.

AFTER THE PRESENTATION

Checking for comprehension

When you present an opinion, it is very important for your classmates to understand what you think. They may want to ask you questions about your opinion. They may also disagree with you.

Therefore, after your presentation, ask your classmates if they have any questions using the language you studied in Unit 1, page 42. Be prepared to give more details on any part of your presentation. Here is some language that you can use.

Responding to questions/comments
That is a good question. What I meant was . . .
Yes, you're right, that is what I think.
No, actually, what I mean is . . .
Thank you for your comment.

Unit 3
Media and Society

In this unit, you will hear people discuss mass media and its effects on our lives. In Chapter 5, you will hear interviews with people about the strengths and weaknesses of the news we get from the Internet, television, and the newspaper. In the lecture, a journalist gives her insight into how an event becomes a news story. In Chapter 6, you will hear people discuss the positive and negative effects of various forms of the media. The lecture is about the dangerous effects that the media can have on us.

Contents

In Unit 3, you will listen to and speak about the following topics.

Chapter 5 Mass Media Today	Chapter 6 Impact of the Media on Our Lives
Interview 1 Problems with TV News	**Interview 1** The Advantages of the Media
Interview 2 Opinions About the Newspapers	**Interview 2** Disadvantages of the Media
Lecture From Event to Story – Making It to the News	**Lecture** Dangers of the Mass Media

Skills

In Unit 3, you will practice the following skills.

Listening Skills	**Speaking Skills**
Listening for main ideas Listening for stressed words Listening for signal words Listening for specific information Listening for tone of voice	Brainstorming about the topic Sharing your opinion Answering multiple-choice questions Applying what you have learned Personalizing the topic Thinking critically about the topic Conducting and presenting your own research
Vocabulary Skills	**Note Taking Skills**
Reading and thinking about the topic Examining vocabulary in context Building background knowledge on the topic Guessing vocabulary from context	Summarizing what you have heard Choosing a format for organizing your notes Recording numerical information Organizing your notes as a map

Learning Outcomes

Prepare and **deliver** an oral presentation as a group on an aspect of media and society

Chapter 5
Mass Media Today

Look at the photograph of people shopping for TVs and answer the questions with a partner.

    1. Have you ever been in a store like this? If so, what was the experience like?

    2. How has increased access to the mass media changed people's lives? How has it changed yours?

1 Getting Started

In this section, you are going to discuss the mass media and think about what makes news interesting and relevant to our lives.

1 Reading and thinking about the topic Ⓥ Ⓢ

A Read the following passage.

The term *mass media* refers to methods of communication with large numbers of people. The rise of the mass media began centuries ago. Gutenberg's printing press first made reading material available in the fifteenth century; in the nineteenth century, the radio began to make audio information available. Television was invented at the beginning of the twentieth century, and by 1950, everybody wanted to have one. The most powerful medium of all, the Internet, appeared in the 1990s, and since then, it has changed our world in ways nobody thought possible. The modern world now depends on extensive communication among people, organizations, and governments.

The media communicates information and entertains us, but it can also be used for many other purposes: to explain, inform, describe, and educate. It can provide companionship, and it can communicate opinions.

However, the rapid growth in the mass media raises questions about its value. For example, some people believe that today's news is not necessarily of good quality. Technological advances give us the impression that we understand the world better because we have access to more information about it, but this is not always true. The information we get may be inaccurate, *biased* (one-sided), or incomplete.

B Answer the questions according to the information in the passage.

1. How is the modern world connected?

2. What does the mass media allow us to do?

3. Why do some people question the value of the mass media?

C Read these questions and share your answers with a partner.

1. What kinds of mass media do you use most?

2. Which advances in technology have helped the mass media evolve?

3. Do you believe that technology helps us understand the world better than we used to? Why or why not?

2 Brainstorming about the topic Ⓢ

When you brainstorm about a topic, you allow yourself to think about it freely and can generate unexpected ideas and reactions. A good way to brainstorm is to think of questions about different aspects of the topic.

A Headlines communicate the main ideas of newspaper articles, but do not follow regular grammatical rules; for example, many verbs are omitted. Read the headlines below. For each headline, write at least two questions that you have about the article. An example has been done for you.

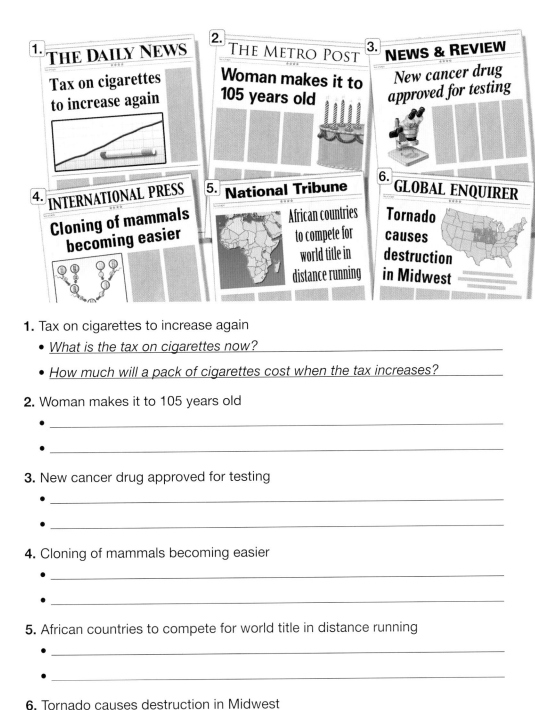

1. Tax on cigarettes to increase again
   - *What is the tax on cigarettes now?*
   - *How much will a pack of cigarettes cost when the tax increases?*

2. Woman makes it to 105 years old
   - _____
   - _____

3. New cancer drug approved for testing
   - _____
   - _____

4. Cloning of mammals becoming easier
   - _____
   - _____

5. African countries to compete for world title in distance running
   - _____
   - _____

6. Tornado causes destruction in Midwest
   - _____
   - _____

B Work with a partner. Share your questions. Then choose some of your questions to share with the class.

3 Listening for specific information Ⓛ Ⓢ

A Read the statistics about how Americans get their news. Then circle whether you are *S* (similar) or *D* (different) from most people.

1. Sixty percent of people prefer to get their news from the Internet than from newspapers or the radio.

   I am . . .   S   D

   The interviewee is . . . S   D

2. If they read a newspaper in print or online, more than 70 percent read only a single article about a news story.

   I am . . .   S   D

   The interviewee is . . . S   D

3. About 25 percent of Americans buy a newspaper every day.

   I am . . .   S   D

   The interviewee is . . . S   D

4. Over a quarter of young people don't read or see any news on a typical day.

   I am . . .   S   D

   The interviewee is . . . S   D

5. When they read a news story, over 75 percent of people share their opinions on a blog or social media site.

   I am . . .   S   D

   The interviewee is . . . S   D

B Listen to an interviewer stop people on the street to ask about their news habits. For each comment, decide whether the speaker is typical or atypical. Then go back to Step A and circle *S* or *D* for each interviewee.

C Compare your responses with other class members.

2 Real-Life Voices

In this section, you will hear five people discuss different perspectives on the news. Carol, a teacher, will explain her mixed feelings about the news she watches on TV. Then a panel of four college students will discuss their feelings about the news.

BEFORE THE INTERVIEWS

Sharing your opinion ⑤

A Read the following quotes about television and news. With a partner, explain what each person is saying. Then decide whether you agree or disagree with the statements.

1. "99.99% of what happens is not on the news."

Marleen Loesje

2. "TV is chewing gum for the eyes."

Frank Lloyd Wright

3. "(Television) is a medium of entertainment which permits millions of people to listen to the same joke at the same time, and yet remain lonesome (lonely)."

T. S. Eliot

4. "I hate television. I hate it as much as peanuts. But I can't stop eating peanuts."

Orson Welles

5. "Television is more interesting than people. If it were not, we would have people standing in the corners of our rooms."

Alan Corenk

6. "Theatre is life. Cinema is art. Television is furniture."

Author Unknown

B Share your most interesting ideas with the class.

INTERVIEW 1 Problems with TV News

1 Examining vocabulary in context ⓥ

Here are some words and phrases from the interview with Carol, printed in **bold** and given in the context in which you will hear them. They are followed by definitions.

The news is based on what's going to keep people **tuned in**: *watching TV*

. . . what's going to keep people tuned in, like **plastic surgery** or **celebrities**: *medical surgery to improve your physical appearance / famous people*

They actually **tease** you to get you to watch the news: *trick, play with*

It's **shallow**: *without serious meaning*

There are these people **doing voice-overs**: *speaking "off-camera" about what the viewer is watching*

It should be quick . . . like **instant gratification**: *immediate satisfaction*

Do you think newspapers . . . give you better news **coverage**?: *reporting*

I *know* I'm being **sucked in!**: *tricked into watching*

2 Answering multiple-choice questions Ⓢ Ⓛ

A Read the items below before you listen to the interview with Carol.

1. According to Carol, news on TV
   a. is mostly about health issues.
   b. is mostly international.
   c. is mostly entertainment.

2. In Carol's opinion, the evening news
   a. is boring to most people.
   b. tricks people into watching.
   c. is an important source of information.

3. Carol thinks that political problems
   a. don't get reported in the way they should be reported.
   b. are not really interesting for most people.
   c. are presented well by TV reporters.

4. Carol believes that most people
   a. are very interested in war and politics.
   b. want information quickly.
   c. don't watch the news.

5. Carol says that if TV news announcers are not physically attractive,
   a. people will not watch TV news.
   b. viewers will complain.
   c. viewers will change channels.

6. According to Carol, newspapers
   a. have a wider audience than TV.
   b. can be read quickly.
   c. present information better.

7. Carol
   a. almost never watches the news on TV.
   b. watches TV news even though she doesn't think it's good.
   c. avoids the mass media.

B Now listen and circle the <u>one</u> correct answer that completes each statement.

C Work with a partner and discuss your answers. Do you agree with Carol?

1 Examining vocabulary in context Ⓥ

Here are some words and phrases from the interviews with the college students, printed in **bold** and given in the context in which you will hear them. They are followed by definitions.

Suppose there's a **disaster** somewhere on the other side of the world: *natural catastrophe, serious problem*

We're **bombarded** by the news 24/7: *surrounded, against our wishes*

I'm constantly checking news **updates**: *the latest information*

If you find out about something **after the fact,** then it's not "news" anymore: *after it happens*

You can **trust** that they are accurate: *really believe*

I think there should be some restrictions on the **paparazzi**: *photographers who take pictures of celebrities*

That's an **invasion of privacy**: *unwelcome attention into private matters*

2 Listening for main ideas Ⓛ Ⓢ

🔊 **A** Look at the chart below and then listen to the interviews. Fill in the chart with the information you hear.

	Is this person interested in the news?		Where does he/she get most of the news (online, TV, etc.)?	What does he/she think? (Write the person's name on all the responses.)
	Yes	No		
Lewis				<u>Lewis</u> 1. Constantly checking the news is a waste of time. _____ 2. Too much news is unhealthy. _____ 3. It's important for us to be able to check many perspectives on the news.
Peter				_____ 4. Keeping up with the news is our responsibility. _____ 5. The news is all one-sided. It should be more well rounded.
Sharon				_____ 6. There is nothing we can do about disasters that happen on the other side of the world. _____ 7. We can't believe everything we read or hear. We must take it with a grain of salt.
Bobbie				_____ 8. There should be more restrictions on the paparazzi.

🔊 **B** Listen to the interviews again. Circle all the answers that apply (*a, b,* or *c*). You may circle more than one answer. Compare your responses with a partner.

1. Lewis says that we need to take a break from the news. What does he recommend doing instead?
   a. We should read more books so that we have a better understanding of the issues.
   b. We should spend more time with our friends and family.
   c. We should travel more and get out into nature.

2. Peter says that we should check the online blogs. He believes that blogs
   a. give us the opportunity to understand the most up-to-date events.
   b. provide different perspectives.
   c. are more fun to read than articles.

3. Sharon says the news is depressing and one-sided. She thinks that
   a. the news should focus on local issues.
   b. human interest stories make people feel more positive.
   c. the Internet does a good job presenting the news.

4. Bobbie speaks about our obsession with celebrities. She thinks that
   a. real people are more interesting than famous people.
   b. the media invade people's privacy.
   c. it is normal to be interested in colorful stories.

3 Listening for stressed words 🅛 🅢

A Read the questions below.

1. The interviewer asks Lewis why he isn't really interested in the news. Lewis replies that he thinks the news is a waste of time. Which word does he stress?
   a. giant   b. can't   c. obsessed

2. The interviewer asks Peter if he reads newspapers online, and Peter says that he does. Which word does he stress?
   a. yes   b. can   c. trust

3. The interviewer asks Sharon why she doesn't turn the news off if she doesn't like it. Sharon admits that she does like the news. Which word does she stress?
   a. admit   b. do   c. like

4. The interviewer says that Bobbie finds the news annoying, and Bobbie agrees. Which word(s) does she stress?
   a. yeah   b. not   c. at all

🔊 **B** Now listen to the excerpts and circle the word(s) that the interviewees stress. Compare your responses with a partner.

1 Summarizing what you have heard Ⓝ Ⓢ

> Summarizing is an important academic skill. In order to paraphrase oral or written material, you must organize information and present it in a clear way.

A With a partner, review the information you have heard. If necessary, listen to the interviews again and take notes.

B Use your notes to write a summary. If you wish, you may use the model below. Fill in the blanks using information from the interviews.

Carol has very strong opinions about the news we get on _____ . She thinks that

_____ . For example, serious stories like _____ and shallow stories like

_____ are presented in the same style. She believes that this is because we are used

to instant _____ , something that doesn't require you to _____ . Newspapers and

the Internet give better coverage, but it takes more time to find good articles, so Carol

_____ .

The panel of college students raises several issues about the news. Some students

think it is very important to keep up with the news because _____ . Other

students believe that the news is not very good because _____ . Instead,

they recommend that we should _____ . However, most of the students say

that they check the news _____ .

2 Sharing your opinion Ⓢ

A Discuss these questions with a small group.

1. It takes a lot of time to keep up with all the developments in current events in our community and around the world. Do you think it is important to keep up with everything that goes on? Why or why not?

2. Most people spend a lot of time online and watching TV. Do you think that the Internet and TV have a positive or negative effect on our ability to read, spend time with friends and family, and do other activities?

3. Do you think that you spend too much time watching TV or going online? How many hours do you spend every day on these activities?

4. Do your parents use the same media as you do to get the news? If not, which type of media do they use? Why?

B Look at the cartoons below. Discuss in a small group what you think the interviewees might say about them.

"Responding to viewer sentiment, we have eliminated world news and expanded our entertainment and sports news."

"I USED TO FETCH THE NEWSPAPER. NOW I JUST ACCESS IT ONLINE AND PRINT IT UP."

3 In Your Own Voice

In this section, you will discuss important events that took place during the twentieth century. Then you will work in groups to discuss more recent news events that you consider important.

Applying what you have learned ⓢ

A Read the following clues about events that the American public and journalists selected in a recent survey as top news stories of the twentieth century. Guess what event is being described. (Check your answers at the bottom of page 100). Then discuss why you think the event was – or was *not* – important.

1903 Two men did something that people thought was impossible.

Event: _The Wright brothers flew an airplane._ _____

1. 1905   A scientist developed a theory that changed our idea of the universe.

Event: _____

2. 1912   There was a big accident at sea.

Event: _____

3. 1920   Women took a big step toward gaining equal rights.

Event: _____

4. 1928   An antibiotic was discovered.

Event: _____

5. 1929   There was a financial crisis in the United States.

Event: _____

6. 1945   The United States used a weapon that had never been tried before.

Event: _____

7. 1963   A famous North American political leader was assassinated.

Event: _____

8. 1969   Explorers took a great step into the unknown.

Event: _____

9. 1989   A new form of mass media was invented.

Event: _____

10. 1997   Scientists made a clone of a mammal.

Event: _____

B Work with a small group. Decide what *you* consider important since 2000. For each category listed below, write an event or the name of a person that was important in relation to the category. Then share your ideas with the class.

1. War or political change: _____

2. Exploration: _____

3. Scientific discovery: _____

4. Accident: _____

5. Disease: _____

6. Other: _____

7. Other: _____

8. Other: _____

C With your small group, complete the following and share your choices with the class.

• An event, discovery, or person from the twentieth century that everyone in the group decides was very important. Give as many details as you can about your selection and explain why it or the person was important.

_____

_____

_____

_____

• An event, discovery, or person in the news today that you think will be considered important in the future. Explain in detail the significance of the person, discovery, or event.

_____

_____

_____

_____

Answers to Step A, page 97
[1] *Albert Einstein developed the theory of relativity.*
[2] *The "unsinkable" ship Titanic sank.*
[3] *Women in the United States won the right to vote.*
[4] *Penicillin was discovered.*
[5] *The U.S. stock market crashed.*
[6] *The United States dropped the atomic bomb.*
[7] *U.S. President John F. Kennedy was assassinated.*
[8] *A human being walked on the moon for the first time.*
[9] *The World Wide Web was invented.*
[10] *Dolly, a sheep, was cloned.*

4 Academic Listening and Note Taking

In this section, you will listen to and take notes on a two-part lecture given by Ms. Sarah Coleman, a journalist. The title of the lecture is "From Event to Story – Making It to the News." Ms. Coleman will explain the steps journalists take and the difficulties they face as they write the stories we read in the newspaper.

1 Building background knowledge on the topic

A Media College is a Web site that provides resources related to the mass media. Read the explanation below about stories that make it to the news.

> **__ Timing**
> The word *news* means exactly that – things that are *new*. If something happened today, it's news. If the same thing happened last week, it's no longer interesting.
> **__ Significance**
> The number of people affected by the story is important. For example, a plane crash in which hundreds of people died is more significant than a crash killing a dozen.
> **__ Proximity**
> Stories that happen near to us have more significance. The closer the story is to home, the more newsworthy It Is. However, proxlmlty doesn't have to mean geographical distance. Stories from countries with which we have a particular bond or similarity have the same effect.
> **__ Prominence**
> Famous people get more coverage just because they are famous. If you break your arm, it won't make the news, but if the queen of England breaks her arm, it's big news.
> **__ Human Interest**
> Human interest stories are a special case. They do not always follow the rules above; for example, they don't date as quickly, they need not affect a large number of people, and it may not matter where in the world the story takes place.

B Work with a partner. Rank the newsworthy factors above from 1 to 5, according to your opinion, with 1 being most important and 5 being least important. Then share your ideas with the class.

2 Listening for signal words

When you are reading a text, you can see how it is organized because it is divided into paragraphs. It may also have section headings. You can also read a text slowly, underline parts you do not understand, and come back to them later.

> In a lecture, it can be more difficult to follow the organization of the speaker's ideas. However, signal words can help you. These words act as markers or sign posts that indicate what kind of information the speaker will give next. In Chapter 1, you learned signal words for introducing examples and definitions. Signal words can be used for other purposes, too. Here are some examples of commonly used signal words.
>
> | | |
> |---|---|
> | To indicate time | *today, nowadays, sometimes, usually, at that point* |
> | To reinforce an idea or introduce a contradiction | *in fact, actually* |
> | To list ideas | *first of all, then, after that, finally* |
> | To introduce a new idea | *and, also, in addition, furthermore* |
> | To introduce an opposite idea | *but, however, on the other hand* |

A The signal words in the left column are used by the lecturer. Match each one with a synonym from the column on the right. Write the correct letter.

____ **1.** Sometimes   **a.** These days

____ **2.** First of all   **b.** But

____ **3.** In fact   **c.** Occasionally

____ **4.** Nowadays   **d.** Generally

____ **5.** However   **e.** To begin with

____ **6.** Usually   **f.** Actually

B Now watch or listen to some parts of the lecture that include the signal words in Step A. As you listen, complete the sentences with the correct word(s). Then compare your answers with a partner.

1. _____ , more than ever before, we are surrounded by news.

2. _____ , so many new stories appear every day that it's impossible to keep up with them!

3. _____ , there are different kinds of journalists.

4. _____ , journalists are called reporters because they "report" the news.

5. _____ , unplanned events are more exciting!

6. _____ , it's important not to report too much personal information or anything that is scandalous.

1 Guessing vocabulary from context V S

A The following items contain important vocabulary from Part 1 of the lecture. Work with a partner. Using the context and your knowledge of related words, take turns guessing the meanings of the words in **bold**.

___ **1.** So many new stories appear every day that it's impossible to **keep up with** them.

___ **2.** She should keep in contact with **civic organizations** in the neighborhood.

___ **3.** The reporter can **anticipate** many of the details.

___ **4.** The reporter will probably see a few lines about the crime in the **police log**.

___ **5.** She can begin to interview **witnesses**.

___ **6.** These details will make the story more **credible**.

___ **7.** It's important not to report anything that is **scandalous**.

___ **8.** She will go back to the **newsroom** to write the story.

___ **9.** She might talk to her **editor** to decide whether she has a good story.

B Work with your partner. Match the vocabulary terms from Step A with their definitions. Write the letter on the line. Check your answers in a dictionary if necessary.

a. supervisor of reporters

b. groups of citizens who organize activities to help and improve the neighborhood

c. read all of, stay informed about

d. know in advance

e. people who see a crime happen

f. shocking, related to scandals

g. easy to believe

h. office at a newspaper where news is prepared for publication

i. record of crimes

2 Choosing a format for organizing your notes

Remember that you do not always have time to choose the best format for organizing your notes clearly when you are listening to a lecture. If the notes you took during a lecture are disorganized, choose an appropriate format and put your notes into that format as soon after the lecture as possible. It is important to have clear notes so that they are useful tools with which you can study. The more you practice taking notes, the easier it will be to choose an appropriate format for them while you listen.

A Look at the three examples of notes on Part 1 of the lecture. Example 1 is an example of a student's disorganized notes on Part 1 of the lecture. They were taken while the lecturer was speaking. Examples 2a and 2b show two different ways that the same information can be organized into clear formats. Example 2a is in column form, and Example 2b is in outline form.

Example 1: Disorganized notes of Part 1 of the lecture, "The Work of a Journalist," that were taken by a student during the lecture

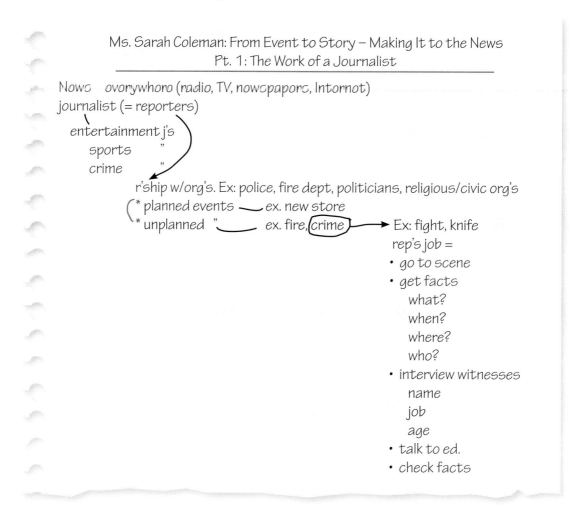

Ms. Sarah Coleman: From Event to Story – Making It to the News
Pt. 1: The Work of a Journalist

News everywhere (radio, TV, newspapers, Internet)
journalist (= reporters)
   entertainment j's
      sports   "
      crime   "
         r'ship w/org's. Ex: police, fire dept, politicians, religious/civic org's
        * planned events — ex. new store
        * unplanned "   ex. fire, crime → Ex: fight, knife
                          rep's job =
                          • go to scene
                          • get facts
                              what?
                              when?
                              where?
                              who?
                          • interview witnesses
                              name
                              job
                              age
                          • talk to ed.
                        • check facts

Example 2a: The first part of the notes is clearly organized in column format based on the information in Example 1.

Ms. Sarah Coleman: From Event to Story – Making It to the News
Part 1: The Work of a Journalist

Main Ideas	Details
News everywhere	radio, TV, newspapers, Internet
Journalists report news	diff' types of journalists (reporters), entertainment, sports, crime
J's establish r'ship w/org's	police/fire depts., politicians, relig/civic org's

Example 2b: The first part of the notes is clearly organized in outline format based on the information in Example 1.

Ms. Sarah Coleman: From Event to Story – Making It to the News
Part 1: The Work of a Journalist

I. News everywhere: radio, TV, newspapers, Internet
II. Journalists report news
   A. diff' types of journalists (reporters)
      1. entertainment
      2. sports
      3. crime
   B. J's establish r'ship w/org's
      1. police/fire depts.
      2. politicians
      3. relig/civic org's

B Now watch or listen to Part 1 of the lecture and take notes on your own paper. Pay attention to the signal words to help you follow the lecture.

C Decide whether you want to organize your notes for Part 1 of the lecture in column format or outline format. Then complete the notes in Example 2a (column format) or 2b (outline format) by adding information from the notes you took in Step B.

1 Guessing vocabulary from context Ⓥ Ⓢ

A The following conversation contains important vocabulary from Part 2 of the lecture. Work with a partner. Using the context and your knowledge of related words, take turns guessing the meanings of the words in **bold**.

Dan: Frankie, did you hear that story about the man who found a memory card in the park?

Frankie: Yes, it was during a big snowstorm, right? But do you think all that information was (1) **accurate**?

Dan: Yes, I'm sure it was because he posted the photographs online to try to find the photographer.

Frankie: Did he find him or her?

Dan: Well, not right away. He got a lot of responses, but he realized that most of the time, he was being (2) **misinformed**. Finally he did manage to find the people in the photo, but guess what? They weren't so happy about seeing their lives spread all over the Internet. I suppose they could have decided to (3) **sue** him for (4) **libel**.

Frankie: Well, I don't think you can post (5) **uncorroborated** facts online, but those were just photos.

Dan: Yeah, you're right. In any case, the story had a happy ending. The guy in the park found the photographer after all.

Frankie: That's a great story. What's the (6) **source** again? Did you say you saw it online?

B Work with your partner. Match the vocabulary terms from Step A with their definitions. Write the word on the line. Check your answers in a dictionary if necessary.

a. given incorrect information _____

b. unchecked _____

c. correct, true _____

d. the crime of telling untrue stories about a person _____

e. bring a legal case against _____

f. people or documents from which you get information _____

2 Choosing a format for organizing your notes

 A Now watch or listen to Part 2 of the lecture and take notes on your own paper. Pay attention to the signal words to help you follow the lecture.

B Complete your organized notes for the lecture by adding information about Part 2 to the column or outline format you chose for Part 1. Then compare your organized notes with a partner.

AFTER THE LECTURE

Applying what you have learned ⓢ Ⓥ

A Work as a class. Choose a day when you will all buy the same edition of the same newspaper. Read the paper before you go to class. Choose three articles, one from each of the following sections of the newspaper.

International news

Local or national news

Arts/Culture/Sports/Entertainment

B Look at the list of adjectives below. Match the adjective on the left with its opposite on the right (an example has been done for you). Then choose the adjectives that best describe the articles you read.

_e_ **1.** uplifting   **a.** full of half-truths

___ **2.** shallow   **b.** objective

___ **3.** one-sided   **c.** well-rounded

___ **4.** biased   **d.** in-depth

___ **5.** trustworthy   **e.** depressing

___ **6.** interesting   **f.** unimportant

___ **7.** important   **g.** boring

C Work in a small group. Take turns sharing your opinion about the articles you have chosen. Give reasons for your choices.

Chapter 6
Impact of the Media on Our Lives

Look at the photograph of a family relaxing at home and answer the questions with a partner.

1. Do you think the family in the photograph is typical of families today? Why or why not?

2. Do you use many different types of media? Which ones do you use the most?

1 Getting Started

In this section, you are going to think about the positive and negative influences of the media. You will also take notes on statistical information about Internet usage around the world.

1 Reading and thinking about the topic ⓥ Ⓢ

A Read the following passage.

During the past century, the mass media has grown in importance. These days, it seems as if everyone owns digital cameras, posts videos, and surfs the Internet. The media connects us across the globe and has become one of society's most important agents of socialization. The Internet, as well as television, radio, newspapers, and other forms of media, has a strong effect on the way we think and act. The media allows us to interact with others, participate in world events, connect with friends and strangers, and keep informed. These abilities are quite new, and they are growing every day.

However, there is disagreement about the effect of the media. For example, not everyone has equal access to the Internet; there is a "digital divide" between those who do and those who do not. In addition, some critics argue that TV invades our privacy and makes us passive, violent, or materialistic. Movies may entertain us, but they may also influence our ideas in ways we do not understand. Phone apps (software applications) open our world, but they may cause us to waste time. We do not yet really understand the extent of their impact on society.

B Answer the following questions according to the information in the passage.

1. Does everyone agree about the kind of effects the media has on society?

2. What are some positive effects of the media? What are some negative effects?

C Read these questions and share your answers with a partner.

1. Do you spend a lot of time surfing the Net, watching TV, or connected to other media? Are you concerned about their possible negative effects? Explain.

2. What steps do you think parents, schools, and the government should take to protect children and adolescents from the negative effects of on-screen violence?

3. Of all the forms of media mentioned in the paragraph, which one seems to have the most influence on you? Why?

2 Personalizing the topic ⑤

A survey published by the Pew Research Center, a group that has studied the impact of the Internet on life in America, includes questions like the ones below. In your group, discuss the questions and your answers using the information you shared above.

1. Some people say they feel overloaded with information these days, considering all the TV news shows, magazines, newspapers, and computer information services. Others say they like having so much information to choose from. Do you feel overloaded, or do you like having so much information available?

2. Overall, do you think that computers and technology give people MORE control over their lives, LESS control over their lives, or don't you think it makes any difference?

3. How much, if at all, have communication and information devices improved your ability to share your ideas with others, do your job, learn new things, and keep in touch with friends and family?

4. Do you like having cell phones and other mobile devices that allow you to be more available to others?

5. When you get a new electronic device, do you usually need someone else to set it up for you or show you how to use it?

6. Do you believe you are more productive because of all your electronic devices?

3 Recording numerical information N L S

It will often be necessary to record the numerical information you hear in conversations, interviews, or lectures. Practice by visualizing numbers when you hear them and then writing them down quickly.

A Work with a partner and look at the map below. It shows the number of Internet users in 11 countries, but it does not include the percentage of Internet users. Guess the missing percentages (an example has been done for you). Write your guesses on the lines next to each area.

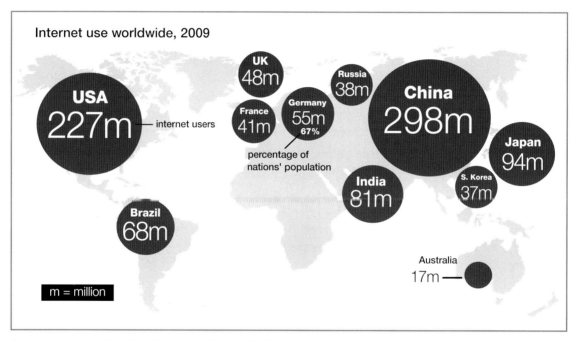

Source: data www.internetworldstats.com. Designed by Greenwich Design, London

B Now listen to a report on Internet usage in each of the countries in Step A. Write the percentages you hear.

C Compare your answers to Step B with your partner. Then compare those answers with your guesses in Step A.

D Discuss the following questions as a class.

1. What information in the report surprises you? Why?
2. In which areas of the world do you think the Internet has the most influence on people? Why? How do you think it influences them?

2 Real-Life Voices

In this section, you will hear four people of different ages give their opinions about the positive and negative effects of various forms of media.

BEFORE THE INTERVIEWS

1 Building background knowledge on the topic

> Remember that it is always useful to learn something about a topic if you are going to discuss it in class. Ways to get background knowledge include:
> * Speaking to people who have personal knowledge about a topic
> * Doing research in a library or online
> * Reading novels, short stories, or poetry about the topic
> * Seeing a movie about the topic

A Read the following poem by Angeline A. Moscatt.

Technology

Technology gave birth to electricity

And illuminated the night skies

But dimmed the shining stars.

Technology brought forth the telephone

Connecting us to loved ones far away

But cell-phone users babble* on

Ignoring the world around them.

Technology advanced step by step

Crossbow** to gunpowder to atomic bomb

That bomb, they say, ended a war –

And the lives of mllions of civilians.

Technology – blessing or curse?

B Moscatt asks whether technology is a blessing or a curse. Work with a partner and discuss the meaning of these two words. If you are not sure, look them up in a dictionary or ask other classmates. Then take turns paraphrasing what Moscatt says about the three examples of technology presented in the poem: electricity, telephones, and weapons.

---

*talk continuously in an excited way without saying anything important
**old-fashioned weapon

2 Personalizing the topic Ⓢ Ⓝ

A Work with a partner and read the following positive and negative effects of the media. Discuss each effect and find an example that you and your partner agree about. Write your examples on the lines.

Positive effects	Example
Keeps the user well informed	<u>Newspapers tell us what is happening in the world.</u>
Is entertaining	_____
Is a good use of time	_____
Is a good form of communication	_____
Allows users to share opinions	_____
_____ (Other)	_____

Negative effects	Example
Causes users to waste time	_____
Encourages violence	_____
Has too much advertising	_____
Encourages people to think alike	_____
(Other)	

B Now look at these forms of communication and entertainment. Choose three. Explain to your partner any positive and negative effects each one has on you.

cell phones	Internet	movies	e-books	video games
Facebook	magazines	newspapers	television	YouTube

INTERVIEW 1   The Advantages of the Media

1 Examining vocabulary in context Ⓥ

Here are some words and phrases from the interview with Kelly, printed in **bold** and given in the context in which you will hear them. They are followed by definitions.

It is so **ingrained** in the world around us: *firmly established*

I can't think of a **realm** of life that computers have not **penetrated**: *area . . . entered*

Sharing of information across the Internet has really **exploded**: *grown in importance*

The online environment is absolutely **central** to our lives: *critically important*

I actually have some **nostalgia** for the pre-technological age: *feeling of affection for the past*

Children now are growing up with a very **skewed** impression of the world: *biased, inaccurate*

. . . a part of our cultural **heritage**: *traditions, beliefs and values*

2 Listening for specific information 🄛 🄝

A Read the questions below before you listen to the interview with Kelly.

1. The interviewer asks Kelly if she thinks the media has a good or bad impact on us. What does Kelly respond?

2. What is the first advantage of the media, in Kelly's opinion? What example does she give?

3. Kelly says that people share more information than ever before. What type of information does she discuss?

4. Kelly says that people are all connected now. What is her opinion about Facebook?

5. Kelly says that she thinks she is very lucky. Why?

B Now listen to the interview. As you listen, take notes on what Kelly says.

C Work with a partner. Use your notes to answer the questions in Step A.

INTERVIEW 2 Disadvantages of the Media

1 Examining vocabulary in context 🅥

Here are some words and phrases from the interview with Nina, Richard, and Orlando, printed in **bold** and given in the context in which you will hear them. They are followed by definitions.

I think we are **brainwashed** by the media: *forced to accept different views, not allowed to think for ourselves*

I also think the media **interferes with** the way we spend our time: *prevents us from using well*

It's wonderful to have the Internet **at your disposal**: *available to you*

I think you have to look at the **trade-off** for whatever you do: *disadvantages*

I **link up with** people: *communicate*

The **developed** world has a great advantage over the **developing** world: *with a high level of industrial development / with a low level of industrial development*

The access is not **even**: *uniform, the same for everyone*

2 Listening for specific information Ⓛ Ⓢ

A Read the summaries below before you listen to the interviews.

1. Nina says that the media makes us *(less able to concentrate / antisocial / unable to spend time working)*. She says that people waste a lot of time online clicking on different links. She also says that while you are online, you are not doing anything else, like *(cooking / cleaning / reading)*. People constantly talk about how much time they waste online.

2. Richard says that the media has a very big trade-off. In fact, he thinks modern technology destroys beauty and meaning in our lives. Therefore, he does not own a *(radio / cell phone / computer)*. On the other hand, some technological innovation is good. Richard says that he thinks although it is not considered a form of media, the jet plane is a positive innovation because it allows people to travel all over the world. In his opinion, traveling improves *(people's education / international communication / people's desire to read)*.

3. Orlando is worried about the digital divide. He says that in *(rural areas / the developing world / older populations)* there is less Internet access. The digital divide can be a problem anywhere. The country that he mentions is *(the United States / India / China)*.

🔊 **B** Now listen to the interviews with Nina, Richard, and Orlando. Circle the correct responses within each summary.

C Compare your answers with a partner.

3 Listening for tone of voice Ⓛ Ⓢ

🔊 **A** Listen to excerpts from the interviews. Circle one item that best completes the statements.

Excerpt 1

Kelly is discussing differences between now and the past. When she speaks about the future of the post office, she sounds

    a. sure of her opinion.

    b. amused.

    c. confident.

Excerpt 2

Nina is talking about how she surfs the Internet. When she explains how long she can spend online, she sounds

    a. serious.

    b. proud.

    c. as if she has mixed feelings.

Excerpt 3

Richard is talking about his feelings toward the media. He says he has to make a confession. He sounds

    a. apologetic.

    b. tired.

    c. confused.

Excerpt 4

Orlando is discussing the digital divide in his country. He sounds

    a. as if the situation is confusing.

    b. worried.

    c. optimistic.

B Compare your answers with a partner. Explain why you chose those answers.

AFTER THE INTERVIEWS

1 Sharing your opinion Ⓢ

A Read the statements below. For each statement, check (✓) whether you agree strongly, agree, are not sure, disagree, or disagree strongly.

	Agree strongly	Agree	Not sure	Disagree	Disagree strongly
1. We are brainwashed by the news we see on TV.					
2. Being online for many hours makes people antisocial.					

	Agree strongly	Agree	Not sure	Disagree	Disagree strongly
3. Discussing books with your friends is a good way to spend time together.					
4. Traveling is a good way to improve international communication.					
5. The digital divide is a big problem.					

B Work in a small group and explain your opinions.

2 Thinking critically about the topic ⓢ ⓝ

A Read the responses to the three questions below. Write your own response to each question.

---

1. Does going online improve people's writing skills?

Adolescent

Yes, because you get a lot of practice when you write online. If I didn't write e-mails, I probably wouldn't write very much at all.

High school teacher

No, it has a bad effect. My students spend hours writing e-mails, but they don't discuss anything important, and they don't use correct English grammar or spelling.

You

_____

2. Is it necessary to have access to the Internet?

Older person in a rural area

No, of course not. I've lived my whole life without the Internet, and I don't need it now.

Person with little Internet access

Yes, but in my country, it's very expensive to go online. That's a big problem, and it stops us from making progress.

You

_____

3. Does the Internet make people smarter?

College student

Absolutely. Sometimes I take my laptop to class and double-check the information my professor is talking about.

College professor

I'm not sure. Sometimes I think it limits learning. Just because people spend a lot of time online, that doesn't mean they are learning anything.

You

_____

B Work with a partner. Take turns sharing your opinions.

3 In Your Own Voice

In this section, you will conduct an experiment about television that was designed by the sociologist Bernard McGrane of Chapman University. It is called "The Un-TV Experiment."

Conducting and presenting your own research

A Read about how to conduct "The Un-TV Experiment."

The Un-TV Experiment

You are going to watch TV for three 10-minute periods. In each of these periods, you will watch a different TV program and do a different task. You will take notes about the tasks. You should sit very quietly and concentrate completely on what you are doing so that you do not make a mistake as you record your data. Make sure that you have everything you need: a comfortable place to sit and write, a pencil or pen, and enough paper.

The Tasks

1. Watch any TV program for 10 minutes. Count how many times you see a technical manipulation (that is, a change) on the screen, including:

   - a cut (the picture changes to another picture, like a slide show)

   - a fade-in or fade-out (one picture slowly changes into another picture)

   - a zoom (the camera moves from a wide view to a close-up view, or from a close-up view to a wide view)

   - a voice-over (a voice explains or comments on what you are watching)

   - another technical change (describe it)

2. Watch a news program for 10 minutes.

   - Count the number of positive images that you see.

   - Count the number of negative images that you see.

   - Make notes about any images that you particularly remember.

3. Watch any TV program for 10 minutes. Do not turn on the sound. As you watch, make notes about these two questions:

   - How interesting is the program?

   - How easy is it to distinguish between the program itself and the commercials?

Now conduct the experiment yourself. A good way to record your results is to use a chart. Your chart should be similar to the one below.

Task 1	Task 2	Task 3
Name of program:	Name of program:	Name of program:
Technical Manipulations (Make a check mark (✓) each time the manipulation occurs.)	Images (Make a check mark (✓) each time the image occurs.) Positive	Negative	Thoughts about: • Interest of program • Ease of distinguishing program from commercials
Cuts:		
Fades:		
Zooms:		
Voice-overs:		
Other:		

B Analyze your data. If you wish, you can compare your results with McGrane's results (see the bottom of this page).

   1. How many technical manipulations did you count?

   2. How many positive images did you see on the news? How many negative ones? What kinds of images do you particularly remember?

   3. How interesting was it to watch TV with no sound? How easy was it to distinguish between the program and the commercials?

C Prepare to describe your experience to a small group. You should be ready to discuss

   • the TV programs you watched for each 10-minute period.

   • the results of the data you gathered during each 10-minute period.

D Discuss these questions in your group or as a class.

   1. Why do you think TV programs have so many technical manipulations?

   2. Did you see more positive or more negative images on the news? Are you surprised at what you saw?

   3. How did the absence of sound affect your viewing?

Results of McGrane's "The Un-TV Experiment"
Task 1: Participants round up to 180 technical manipulations in 10 minutes. **Task 2:** Participants found a huge number of negative images. **Task 3:** Participants found that 10 minutes of sound-free TV was boring. Many of them lost their concentration and had difficulty distinguishing between the program and the commercials.

4 Academic Listening and Note Taking

In this section, you will hear and take notes on a two-part lecture given by Dedra Smith, a media expert who conducts workshops about media and society. The title of the lecture is "Dangers of the Mass Media." Ms. Smith will describe what she believes are some harmful effects of the media today.

BEFORE THE LECTURE

1 Personalizing the topic Ⓢ

A According to experts, Americans spend a lot of time online. Some people say they spend up to 8 hours a day! What are people doing online? Look at the following chart produced by the Nielsen Company, which monitors media use.

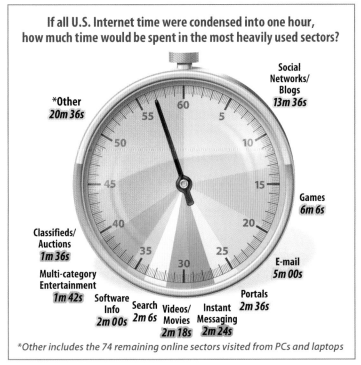

Source: Nielsen

B Work with a partner. Discuss how you spend your time online. Do you spend more or less time on the activities listed above than the typical Internet user?

2 Organizing your notes as a map Ⓝ Ⓛ

> One way of taking notes is called *mapping.* In this method, you write the main idea on your paper and draw lines out to related points. As you take notes, you can show connections between different parts of the lecture by adding lines.

A Look at the following map of excerpts from Part 1 of Ms. Smith's lecture.

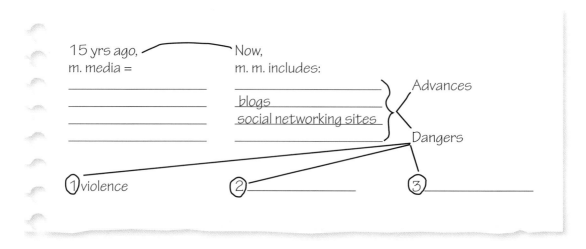

 B Now watch or listen to the excerpts and complete the map.

C Compare your map with a partner.

LECTURE PART 1   Violence, Passivity, and Addiction

1 Guessing vocabulary from context Ⓥ Ⓢ

A The following conversations contain important vocabulary from Part 1 of the lecture. Work with a partner. Using the context and your knowledge of related words, take turns guessing the meanings of the words in **bold**.

Conversation One

Christie: Hey, Dwane. I'm so upset. Did you read what just happened downtown?

Dwane: No! What happened?

Christie: Some kids set a (1) **subway booth** on fire.

Dwane: That's terrible! I wasn't (2) **aware** of anything like that! Where did you see that story – on a blog?

Christie: Yeah, and (3) **tragically**, these kids had seen a movie about a story like that.

Dwane: Parents should be more (4) **conscious** of what their children watch. Kids are really (5) **susceptible** to the negative images they see.

Conversation Two

Thomas: Alice, what time is it?

Alice: Uh . . . it's past 10.

Thomas: Ten? How long have I been (6) **wandering** around cyberspace?

Alice: At least two hours. I told you that the media can be very (7) **addictive**!

Thomas: Well, at least it's still time for the news on TV. Let's turn it on.

Alice: You shouldn't spend so much time connected to your electronic devices. They say it makes people too (8) **passive**. Let's play cards instead.

B Work with your partner. Match the vocabulary terms from Step A with their definitions. Write the vocabulary word on the line. Check your answers in a dictionary if necessary.

a. hard to stop or give up _____

b. office that sells subway or metro cards or tokens _____

c. informed about _____

d. likely to be affected by _____

e. sadly _____

f. moving with no clear direction or purpose _____

g. not wanting to do anything; inactive _____

h. aware _____

2 Organizing your notes as a map Ⓝ Ⓛ

A Look at the following map. It is a map for all of Part 1 of the lecture. Notice that you already know some of the missing information because you listened to excerpts from Part 1 in the note-taking task on page 120. Copy your answers from that task onto the appropriate lines in this map.

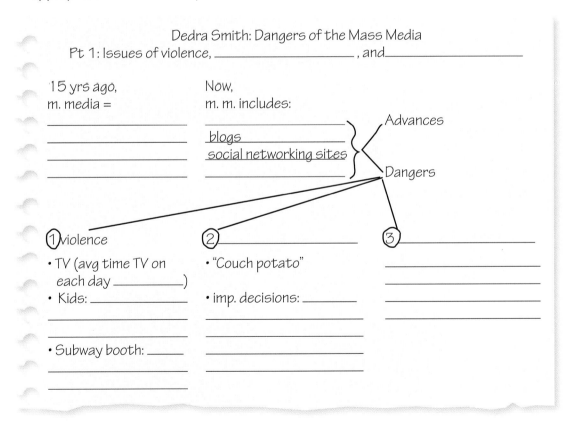

Dedra Smith: Dangers of the Mass Media

Pt 1: Issues of violence, _____ , and _____

15 yrs ago,
m. media =
_____
_____
_____
_____

Now,
m. m. includes:
_____
blogs
social networking sites
_____

Advances

Dangers

①violence
• TV (avg time TV on each day _____)
• Kids: _____
_____
• Subway booth: _____
_____
_____

②_____
• "Couch potato"
• imp. decisions: _____
_____
_____

③_____
_____
_____
_____
_____
_____

🔊 **B** Now watch or listen to Part 1 of the lecture and complete the map.

C Compare your map with a partner.

1 Guessing vocabulary from context Ⓥ Ⓢ

A The following items contain important vocabulary from Part 2 of the lecture. Work with a partner. Using the context and your knowledge of related words, take turns guessing the meanings of the words in **bold.**

___ **1.** The content . . . is just an excuse, or a kind of **wrapping**, for the advertising.

___ **2.** There is an essential **marketing** relationship among the media, the advertiser, and the user.

___ **3.** Even **print media . . .** has a high percentage of ads.

___ **4.** We are used to being bombarded by **endless** commercials.

___ **5.** Many of us use our remote controls to **zap out** the advertising with the "mute" button.

___ **6.** Advertisers . . . gather statistical data about people like you – **potential consumers**.

___ **7.** Information about you can be **compiled** and sold to other companies.

___ **8.** You can be **tracked** if you make a few visits to any Web site.

B Work with your partner. Match the vocabulary terms from Step A with their definitions. Write the letter on the line. Check your answers in a dictionary if necessary.

a. cover

b. get rid of

c. gathered

d. newspapers and magazines

e. followed

f. buying and selling

g. people who might buy something

h. with no limit

2 Organizing your notes as a map Ⓝ Ⓛ Ⓢ

A Look at the following notes from Part 2 of the lecture. The note taker has just written down the words that he or she heard, without taking the time to organize them clearly. Think about the best way to organize this information in a map.

4. increase in advertising

   past different, now ads everywhere (TV, mags . . .)

   marketing – media ←→ advertiser ←→ user

   TV – endless commercials

   Remote no help because product placement: soft drinks, shoes, etc.

5. not just advertising but invasion of privacy

   get info about you . . . credit cards . . . junk mail . . . address . . . phone calls . . .

   Internet: collect info about you . . . your habits

   Message: having more = success

   True? Are we what we buy?

B As you watch or listen to Part 2 of the lecture, take notes on your own paper.

C Use your notes to help you make a complete map of the lecture. You can either copy the map of Part 1 on page 121 on your own paper and add to it, or make another map for Part 2 in your own style.

D Compare your map with a partner.

E Practice giving an oral summary of advertising and invasion of privacy with your partner.

Applying what you have learned Ⓢ Ⓝ

A Look at the left column below. It shows a list of activities in a day in the life of an imaginary college student. Work with a partner and try to think of every situation in which the student is being targeted as a possible consumer. Write as many ideas as you can in the column on the right. Use your own paper if necessary.

Time	Day in the life of a student	Marketing messages
7:00 a.m.	Clock radio goes off; student stays in bed	*Student hears several commercials.*
7:30	Gets up and showers	
7:50	Gets dressed	
8:00	Eats breakfast	
8:15	Checks e-mail	
8:30	Turns on TV to check weather	
8:45	Looks at newspaper and then leaves house	
9:00	Goes into a local shop to buy pens	
9:15	Takes bus or subway to school	
12:30 p.m.	Eats lunch at a fast-food restaurant	
1:00	Goes to library	
3:30	Buys book in bookstore using a credit card	
4:00	Goes to the movies with friends	
7:30	Returns home, cooks dinner	
9:00	Gets a phone call from a telemarketer	
10:00	Goes online	
11:00	Watches sports on TV	
12:00 a.m.	Goes to bed	

B Discuss these questions with your partner.

1. Compare your life with the student in Step A. Do you have more advertising in your life? Less? The same?

2. Do you think that you are influenced by advertising? Why or why not?

3. Are you worried about the effects of the media? If so, what do you think is the worst effect?

Unit 3 Academic Vocabulary Review

This section reviews the topics and vocabulary from Chapters 5 and 6. For a complete list of all the Academic Word List words in this book, see the Appendix on pages 181–182.

A Look at the list of words. Write the part(s) of speech each word represents: V for verb, A for adjective, N for noun, or O for other. Use your dictionary if necessary. Then compare your answers with the class.

Academic word	Part(s) of speech	Academic word	Part(s) of speech
1. access		9. overall	
2. consumer		10. perspective	
3. contradict		11. relevant	
4. innovation		12. require	
5. issue		13. restrict	
6. manipulate		14. select	
7. negative		15. survey	
8. objective		16. theory	

B Use a form of the words below to complete the news reports.

1. *Celebrity wedding plans revealed*
The breaking news today is the upcoming marriage of April Lee and George Davis, stars of the recent hit show *Love in Paris*. Fans are flooding online to win tickets to the event, which will be held in central London. _____ to the area is going to be severely _____ . Winners will be chosen on Monday. If you are one of the lucky ones to get _____ , you will be _____ to bring official ID to the event.

> **access**   **require**   **restrict**   **select**

2. *Cholesterol levels rising*
_____ , be careful: high levels of fat in prepared food can lead to harmful cholesterol levels. Fatty foods have a strong impact on the body's ability to function well – and that's not just the _____ of a few doctors. Most medical professionals believe that we should be eating more fruits and vegetables and that _____ , we should spend more time exercising and less time eating junk food. This advice is _____ to all of us.

> **consumer**   **overall**   **perspective**   **relevant**

3. *New smartphone released*
_____ show that we're all interested in more effective phone service. That's why there will be a lot of excitement over next week's release of the fastest smartphone on the market. "Let there be no mistake," said one media critic. "_____ is the

name of the game. This is the best product available, and that's an honest opinion."
Not everyone agrees with his opinion, of course. Users of other models say that
public opinion is being _____ by the media, and that the company's marketing
messages are not _____ .

manipulate	innovation	objective	survey

4. *Bees disappearing across the globe*

Scientists are seeing a dramatic decline in the number of bees worldwide. This

_____ has become more serious in recent years. Says beekeeper Sam Adams:

"There are many _____ about why bees are disappearing. I'm feeling pretty

_____ about the whole situation. The experts are all _____ each other, so in my

opinion, nobody knows why this problem is happening."

contradict	issue	negative	theory

C Use the academic vocabulary from A above to answer the following questions, in pairs
or as a class.

The news

1. Where do people usually get their news?
2. What are some opinions about the quality of the news?
3. What are some factors that make an event "newsworthy"?

The work of a journalist

4. What does a journalist's work involve?
5. What are the steps involved in reporting on an event?
6. How is the journalist's job different today than it was in the past?

The growth of the media

7. What kinds of media are popular these days?
8. What do people use media to do?
9. How is technology linked to the media?

Dangers of the media

10. What is the digital divide, and why is it important?
11. What are some dangers of the mass media?
12. Why do some people say it is unreasonable to criticize the media?

Oral Presentation

In academic courses, professors sometimes ask students to give group presentations on a topic. Group presentations are especially interesting when the topic involves different areas, people, dates, issues, or other categories. Group presentations tend to be longer than individual presentations and need to be structured carefully so that they are informative and interesting.

BEFORE THE PRESENTATION

1 Choose a topic

Work in a small group. Choose one of the following topics to research and present to the class. You should have enough information to make a 10-minute presentation.

1. Events in the news this week
2. Celebrities who contribute to a good cause
3. Stories in different sections of a newspaper
4. Key dates in the digital revolution
5. Different types of new media
6. Different users of media
7. Online resources for studying people's media habits
8. Other topic (Choose a topic that can be broken down into several areas.)

2 Organize your presentation

To make an effective group presentation, everyone in the group should work together as a team and contribute to the success of the project. Here are some guidelines.

- Choose one person to be a coordinator. The coordinator should make sure that each person in the group has different responsibilities and that the work is distributed equally.
- Gather enough background information to make your presentation interesting and convincing.
- Make an outline of what you want to say and prepare an introduction.
- Divide your ideas so that each person has something different to say.
- Practice your presentation together several times before you give it in class.

Here is a possible plan for a presentation.

Coordinator: Introduces the presenters and the topic (Events in the News This Week); tells the class about the sources the team used and how they chose their stories
Person 2: Summarizes an important international news event
Person 3: Speaks about a human interest story
Person 4: Discusses an editorial comment
Person 5: Talks about one of the most e-mailed articles
Coordinator: Asks the class if they have any questions or comments

DURING THE PRESENTATION

Time your part of the presentation carefully so that each person has enough time to explain his or her ideas. The coordinator should make sure that the group's presentation goes smoothly from one person to the other and can help to keep time.

Here are some expressions to help keep the class informed about your presentation.

So that's the end of my comments . . .
And now my partner, (name), will talk to you about . . .
Thank you for listening. Now I'd like to introduce . . .
The next presenter is . . .

AFTER THE PRESENTATION

Performing a self-assessment

In your group, answer the questions below. Discuss what you did well and also how you would like to improve future presentations. Make sure you are respectful, supportive, and honest.

Did your group . . .

1. divide up the work evenly?
3. practice speaking together?
2. do enough research on the topic?
4. pay attention to the other group members?

Did you . . .

1. speak clearly and concisely?
3. work with the other team members?
2. make sure to respect the time limit?
4. take responsibility for your part of the project?

Here is some language you can use.

I think that you (name) were very clear when you talked about (topic).
I thought the class reacted . . . (describe how)
I would like to know what the class thought when we . . . (describe something you did)
I think we can improve by . . . (explain how)
I find it difficult to . . . (explain something that you find challenging)

Unit 4
Breaking the Rules

This unit examines crime and punishment. In Chapter 7, you will hear interviews with parents who are concerned about crime. You will also hear from two crime victims. Then you will listen to a lecture on types of crime and methods of solving crime. In Chapter 8, you will hear interviews on how society should try to keep crime rates low, including ways to prevent crime and punish criminals. The lecture is on one of the most controversial topics in the United States today – the death penalty.

Contents

In Unit 4, you will listen to and speak about the following topics.

Skills

In Unit 4, you will practice the following skills.

 Listening Skills

Listening for details
Listening for tone of voice
Listening for opinions
Listening for main ideas
Listening for contrasting ideas

 Speaking Skills

Brainstorming about the topic
Sharing your opinion
Examining graphics
Answering true/false questions
Reacting to what you have heard
Personalizing the topic
Thinking critically about the topic
Applying what you have heard
Supporting your opinion

 Vocabulary Skills

Reading and thinking about the topic
Building background knowledge on the topic
Examining vocabulary in context
Guessing vocabulary from context

 Note Taking Skills

Clarifying your notes
Using your notes to answer test questions
Applying what you have learned
Recording numerical information
Using your notes to ask questions and make comments
Summarizing what you have heard

Learning Outcomes

Prepare and **deliver** an oral presentation on a topic related to crime

Chapter 7
Crime and Criminals

Look at the photograph of a crime scene and answer the questions with a partner.

    1. What do you think is happening in this photo?

    2. Would you like to have a career in criminal justice? Why or why not?

1 Getting Started

In this section, you are going to discuss deviance, crime, and types of crime. You will also listen to some news reports about different types of crime.

1 Reading and thinking about the topic Ⓥ Ⓢ

A Read the following passage.

    In all societies, some behaviors conform to what is expected while other behaviors are thought of as *deviant* (people think they are unacceptable). Some, but not all, deviant behavior is illegal. A *crime* is a deviant act that is prohibited by the law.

    The U.S. legal system recognizes two main categories of crime. *Felonies* are serious crimes; *misdemeanors* are less serious. But there are other ways to describe different types of crime, too. For example, crime can be violent or nonviolent. There is "white-collar crime" (crime committed by professionals) and "blue-collar crime," which includes both small crimes such as shoplifting and also serious crimes such as robbery and murder. There are also modern crimes that have been made possible by technology, such as cybercrime (crimes connected with the Internet), and "crimes of passion." Public interest in crime is very strong.

    However, it is difficult to know how many crimes are committed because most crimes are not reported, and most criminals are not caught. Many crimes are also controversial. There is a lot of disagreement about why crime happens, who is responsible, and how society should deal with it.

B Answer the questions according to the information in the passage.

    1. What is deviant behavior? Is deviant behavior always a crime?

    2. What are two main categories of crime?

    3. What makes it difficult to know how many crimes are committed?

C Read the questions and share your answers with a partner.

    1. What different types of crime do you know about?

    2. How is crime punished in your community?

2 Brainstorming about the topic Ⓢ Ⓝ

A Work with a partner. Look at the word map below. Its branches show different aspects of crime, such as types of crime, causes and effects of crime, personal experiences with crime, and punishments for crime. You can add other aspects of crime that occur to you. Write your ideas on the word map. Add as many lines to the word map as you wish.

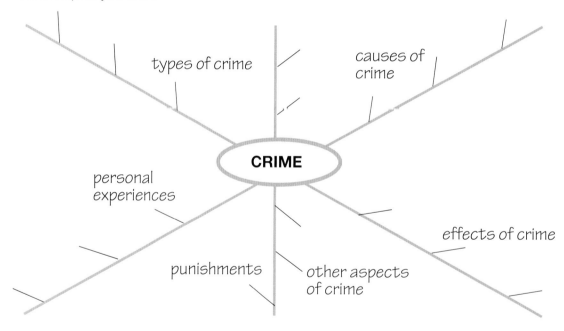

B Share your ideas with another pair of classmates.

3 Building background knowledge: Technical terms

Many fields of study have technical terms that you need to know in order to understand and discuss topics in that field.

A Read the technical terms for various types of crime and their definitions (in parentheses) in the left column of the chart. Then listen to a series of radio crime reports. As you listen, write the number of the report next to the type of crime that is being reported.

Type of crime	Report number
Arson (setting property on fire)	
Burglary (going into a building to steal something)	
Motor vehicle theft (stealing a car)	
Murder (killing someone, also called "homicide")	
Rape (forcing someone to have sexual relations)	
Shoplifting (stealing from a store)	
Weapons possession (having a weapon without a license)	

B Compare your answers with a partner.

4 Sharing your opinion ⓢ

A Work in a small group. Look at the photograph and discuss whether you think it shows deviant behavior. Explain the reasons for your answers.

B Read the list of deviant behaviors below. Number them in order of how wrong or unacceptable they are: 1 = most unacceptable; 8 = most acceptable.

____ Getting into the bus or subway without paying a fare

____ Taking paper or office supplies from your school or workplace

____ Receiving too much change from a cashier for a purchase and not returning it

____ Buying counterfeit goods, such as pocketbooks, shoes, or DVDs

____ Making a copy of a CD and giving it to your friends

____ Damaging someone's parked car and not leaving your contact information

____ Keeping an item that was delivered to you by mistake

____ Pretending to be sick so that you can get medicine from a doctor

C Discuss with your group whether you would consider any of the behaviors in Step B to be crimes.

2 Real-Life Voices

In this section, you will hear four people share their opinions about crime. First, you will hear Evelina and Arpad, the parents of a young child, discuss their fears about crime in society. Then Gail, a professional dancer, and Tom, a graduate student, will talk about being crime victims.

Examining graphics ⓢ

A Work with a partner. Look at the two pie charts below that classify arrests in the United States today. The chart on the left classifies arrests by age group. The chart on the right classifies arrests by gender. Fill in the chart legends with your guesses about the age and gender of people arrested.

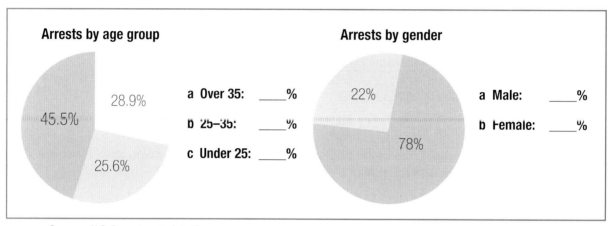

Arrests by age group

28.9%
45.5%
25.6%

a **Over 35:** ____%

b **25–35:** ____%

c **Under 25:** ____%

Arrests by gender

22%
78%

a **Male:** ____%

b **Female:** ____%

Source: U.S. Department of Justice

B Check your responses using the answer key at the bottom of page 135. Were your guesses correct? Does any of the information surprise you?

1 Examining vocabulary in context Ⓥ

Here are some words and phrases from the interview with Evelina and Arpad, printed in **bold** and given in the context in which you will hear them. They are followed by definitions.

I've never actually been **struck** by crime: *personally affected*

I see big groups of kids **roaming** the streets: *walking around with no clear purpose*

If it's a **rowdy** teenage group: *noisy, wild*

I've never seen anyone with a gun – and **much less** seen a shooting: *even less, certainly haven't*

It's very **random**; that's what worries me: *without any definite pattern*

The **bullet** struck him in the leg: *small metal object fired from a gun*

Kids who get into **gangs** don't have that much contact with other people: *groups of young people who are involved in antisocial or illegal activities*

It's a **recipe for disaster**: *situation that will lead to serious trouble*

The government has such a **slack** attitude toward guns: *lazy, not interested*

2 Answering true/false questions Ⓢ Ⓛ Ⓝ

A Read the following statements before you listen to the interview with Evelina and Arpad.

___ **1.** Evelina is concerned about the crime news that she sees on TV.

___ **2.** Arpad is not bothered by loud groups of teenagers on the street.

___ **3.** Evelina is worried about the availability of drugs.

___ **4.** Arpad says that someone was recently shot in a local restaurant.

___ **5.** Evelina says that parents need to have more contact with their children.

___ **6.** Arpad blames the high levels of crime on the level of unemployment.

___ **7.** Arpad thinks that teachers have the main responsibility for teaching values to children.

___ **8.** Arpad supports gun control by the government.

B Listen to the interview and take notes. Use your notes to respond to the statements above. Write *T* (true) or *F* (false).

C Compare your answers with a partner.

INTERVIEW 2   Being the Victim of a Crime

Gail often works late at night. Once some young men robbed her, and she explains what happened. Tom talks about being the victim of burglars and pickpockets.

1 Examining vocabulary in context Ⓥ

Here are some words and phrases from the interview with Gail and Tom, printed in **bold** and given in the context in which you will hear them. They are followed by definitions.

Once I was **mugged** by some young kids: *attacked and robbed*

Kids like that don't need **prosecuting**: *being charged with a crime and taken to court*

Kids are so **vulnerable**: *easily influenced*

It's almost a **macho** type of thing: *strong and manly*

The apartment was **ransacked**: *broken into, searched, and left in a messy condition*

I lost **irreplaceable** personal items: *something you can never get again*

It's like a feeling of **violation**: *invasion*

I've had things taken by **pickpockets**: *thieves who steal things out of pockets or bags, especially in crowds*

It had **symbolic** value: *emotional, sentimental*

2 Listening for details 🅛 🅢

A Read the following questions and the three possible answer choices.

1. Where was Gail mugged?
   a. on the street
   b. outside a theater
   c. at home

2. Which items of clothing was Gail wearing?
   a. a scarf
   b. gloves
   c. a hat

3. About how old were the boys who asked her for money?
   a. 13
   b. 14
   c. 15

4. What did Gail wonder?
   a. What would their teachers say?
   b. Who's responsible for these children?
   c. What will happen if I don't give them my money?

5. In Gail's opinion, what did the boys need?
   a. good parenting
   b. supervision
   c. more self-esteem

6. What was taken from Tom's apartment?
   a. money
   b. a camera
   c. paperwork

7. How did Tom feel?
   a. angry
   b. helpless
   c. scared

8. What did pickpockets take from Tom on the subway?
   a. his watch
   b. a letter from his girlfriend
   c. his wallet

9. Did Tom call the police?
   a. yes
   b. no
   c. he can't remember

B Now listen to the interview and respond to the questions. One, two, or three answers could be correct. Check your answers with a partner.

3 Listening for tone of voice 🅛 🅢

🔊 **A** Listen to excerpts from the interviews with Evelina, Arpad, Gail, and Tom. How do the interviewees sound? You can choose an adjective or adjectives from the box below, or add your own.

angry	resigned	serious	thankful
patient	sad	surprised	thoughtful

Excerpt One

The interviewer asks Evelina if she worries about the level of crime in the city.
When Evelina responds, she sounds _____ .

Excerpt Two

The interviewer asks Arpad if he is worried about violence.
When Arpad responds, he sounds _____ .

Excerpt Three

The interviewer asks Gail what happened when she was mugged.
When Gail responds, she sounds _____ .

Excerpt Four

The interviewer asks Tom if he was scared when his apartment was robbed.
When Tom responds, he sounds _____ .

B Compare your answers with a partner. Give reasons for your choices.

AFTER THE INTERVIEWS

1 Reacting to what you have heard 🅢

Work in a small group. Read the questions below and share your responses with your group.

1. Some of the interviewees are very worried about crime. Are you worried about it?
2. Can people avoid becoming the victims of crime? If so, how?
3. Do you think the media makes us believe society is more dangerous than it actually is?
4. Who should be responsible for reducing crime, in your opinion?

2 Examining graphics Ⓢ

A Look at the graph below. It shows the percentage of selected crimes reported to the police.

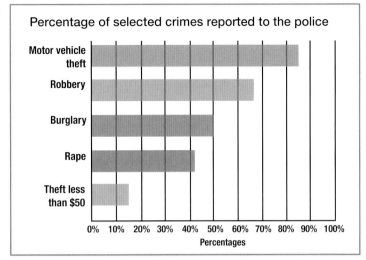

Percentage of selected crimes reported to the police

Motor vehicle theft
Robbery
Burglary
Rape
Theft less than $50

0% 10% 20% 30% 40% 50% 60% 70% 80% 90% 100%
Percentages

Source: Sourcebook of Criminal Justice Statistics

B Discuss these questions with a partner. Base your answers on the graph in Step A and your own ideas.

1. Which crimes get reported most frequently?
2. Which crimes are reported least frequently?
3. How do you explain the fact that people report some crimes less often than others?
4. According to official statistics, it is estimated that less than half of all crimes are reported to the police. Why do you think this is true?

3 Personalizing the topic Ⓢ

Imagine that you are in situations like Gail and Tom. What would you do? Circle the letters of all the answers that apply. Discuss your responses with a partner.

1. You are alone in a city, and it is late. You need to get home. Would you . . .
   a. take the bus or train, even if you have to wait a long time?
   b. walk home quickly but without being very concerned?
   c. decide not to go home, but to stay with some friends nearby?

2. If a stranger approached you, would you . . .
   a. act calmly and talk to the stranger?
   b. run away as fast as you could?
   c. ignore the person and keep on walking?

3. If someone told you to hand over your money, would you . . .
   a. agree to give the person your money?
   b. say nothing and pretend not to hear?
   c. refuse to give the person the money?

4. If a person stole a small amount of money from you, would you . . .
   a. be very hurt and afraid?
   b. feel sorry for the criminal?
   c. feel angry about what happened?

3 In Your Own Voice

In this section, you will discuss various aspects of crime and criminals. You will practice speaking about your knowledge, ideas, and values. Divide the class into two groups: Group A and Group B. Group A, look at this page. Group B, use page 141.

Sharing your opinion: Group A Ⓢ

A Look at the chart below. It has questions about different aspects of crime and criminals. Circulate among your classmates, using the game board to ask questions (one question per classmate). If your classmate can give you a well-developed answer to a question – not just one sentence – write the name of the classmate in that box and make some brief notes about the answer. Listen carefully because your classmate may have a different set of questions. When you complete three boxes across and three down, stop the activity.

Find someone who . . .		
has a recommendation about how to reduce the level of crime in society.	has an opinion about what causes crime.	knows the name and story of a famous criminal in history.
has seen a crime movie and can tell you the story.	can offer an explanation of the high level of violent crime in the United States.	has seen a crime report on TV and can tell you what happened.
can comment on one of the following types of crime: * crimes committed by adolescents * crimes committed by women	knows a police officer and can tell you about his or her job.	has been a witness to a crime and is prepared to tell the story of what happened.

B Work in a small group. Take turns explaining some of the answers you got from your classmates. Then choose the most interesting answer in your group and share it with the class.

Sharing your opinion: Group B Ⓢ

A Look at the chart below. It has questions about different aspects of crime and criminals. Circulate among your classmates, using the game board to ask questions (one question per classmate). If your classmate can give you a well-developed answer to a question – not just one sentence – write the name of the classmate in that box and make some brief notes about the answer. Listen carefully because your classmate may have a different set of questions. When you complete three boxes across and three down, stop the activity.

Find someone who . . .		
thinks the community he or she lives in is dangerous and can explain why.	has an opinion about what makes a person break the law.	has read about a crime in the newspaper or online and can tell you what the article said.
has read a crime novel and can tell you the story.	knows a lawyer and can tell you about his or her job.	can describe a really well-publicized crime – something that dominated the newspapers and TV and captured the public's interest.
can comment on one of the following types of crime: * Internet crime * organized crime	can describe an activity that is considered illegal but that the person believes should be legalized.	has been on a jury and can tell you about the experience.

B Work in a small group. Take turns explaining some of the answers you got from your classmates. Then choose the most interesting answer in your group and share it with the class.

4 Academic Listening and Note Taking

In this section you will hear and take notes on a two-part lecture by Professor Michael Anglin, a lawyer. The title of the lecture is "Crime and Ways of Solving Crime." Professor Anglin will review categories and types of crime, and go on to discuss some methods of solving crime.

BEFORE THE LECTURE

1 Organizing vocabulary: Technical terms Ⓥ Ⓝ

> One way to become familiar with the technical vocabulary of a particular subject is to try organizing that subject into word groups. Surprisingly, you might find that you understand more than you think you do.

Work with a partner. Look at the word map for organizing different kinds of crime vocabulary. Then read the list of words at the top of page 143 and write the words in the appropriate word groups on the map. Use a dictionary if necessary. Then add as many new words to the word map as you can.

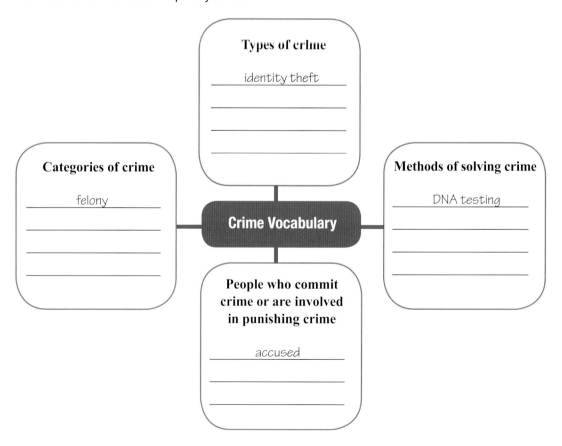

Types of crime
identity theft

Categories of crime
felony

Crime Vocabulary

Methods of solving crime
DNA testing

People who commit crime or are involved in punishing crime
accused

blue-collar crime	fare evasion	jury	profiling
crime hotline	felony	kidnapping	psychological
defendant	fingerprinting	misdemeanor	white-collar crime
DNA testing	judge	pickpocketing	witness

2 Clarifying your notes

If you find that there are some parts of a lecture that you cannot understand because the lecturer is speaking quickly or the ideas and vocabulary are difficult, do not panic!

Develop a system that you can use during a lecture for noting down ideas or words that you need to check. The fastest way is to use circles, question marks, or asterisks (*) to mark problem items. You can use this method during the lecture itself.

After the lecture, make notes of your questions in the margin. Your questions could involve minor items, such as spelling, or major items, such as comprehension of an idea or opinion.

Take the time to clarify any information that you do not understand. Most lecturers will encourage you to ask questions. Otherwise, you can try to clarify anything that you do not understand by asking your classmates, looking in your textbook, or doing research in a library or online.

A Look at the student's notes below. They are notes on the beginning of Professor Anglin's lecture. The circles, question marks, and asterisks indicate things that the student has not understood. Now look at the right side of the page and notice the questions about these things that the student has written.

Prof. Michael Anglin: Crime and Ways of Solving Crime

I. Crime – 2 cats
   A. Felonies and Misdimors (sp??)   spelling?
   B. mis => 15/50?? days & <1 yr.   15 or 50 days?
II. Legal process
   A. Accused goes thru legal process
   B. Goes to judge or jury
   C. ****decides punishment   who decides: judge or jury?

B Watch or listen to an excerpt from the lecture and try to answer the student's questions. Ask other classmates for clarification, if necessary.

1 Guessing vocabulary from context Ⓥ Ⓢ

A The following conversation contains important vocabulary from Part 1 of the lecture. Work with a partner and read the conversation aloud. Using the context and your knowledge of related words, take turns trying to guess the meanings of the words in **bold.**

> **Peter:** I'm taking a really interesting class on crime. We were discussing misdemeanors.
>
> **Lisbeth:** What exactly are misdemeanors?
>
> **Peter:** Well, like . . . graffiti, or dangerous driving. They're crimes – more serious than getting a parking ticket, for example. But not as serious as felonies.
>
> **Lisbeth:** What's a felony? Is that like (1) **robbery**?
>
> **Peter:** Yeah, (2) **broadly** speaking, robbery is (3) **classified** as a felony. It's serious – more serious than, say, pickpocketing, because it probably involves breaking into a building or attacking a person on the street. Sometimes it involves guns, too. And it carries a term of (4) **imprisonment** of at least a year.
>
> **Lisbeth:** Mmm, that's scary. Hey, I'm confused about white-collar crime, too. What is that?
>
> **Peter:** Well, blue-collar crime is called "crime on the street," but they call white-collar crime "crime in a suit." You know why? Because the criminals are people of (5) **high social status** . . . White-collar crime includes things like (6) **tax fraud** and (7) **embezzlement**, as well as identity theft.
>
> **Lisbeth:** Do those crimes always get (8) **prosecuted**?
>
> **Peter:** No, according to what I've read, they don't. My professor said that "the big fish get away, but the small fish get caught." I think that's sad.

B Work with your partner. Match the vocabulary terms from Step A with their definitions. Write the word(s) on the line. Check your answers in a dictionary if necessary.

a. taken to court _____

b. stealing money from the place where you work _____

c. loosely, generally _____

d. cheating on your taxes _____

e. important position in society _____

f. time spent in prison (jail) _____

g. using force to steal _____

h. organized, categorized _____

2 Clarifying your notes

 A Watch or listen to Part 1 of the lecture and take notes on your own paper. Use circles, question marks, or asterisks to signal any parts of the lecture that you do not understand. Then write your questions in the margin.

B Clarify your notes by finding the answers to your questions.

C Compare your notes with a partner.

LECTURE PART 2   Ways of Solving Crime

1 Guessing vocabulary from context

The following items contain important vocabulary from Part 2 of the lecture. Work with a partner. Using the context and your knowledge of related words, circle the letter of the best synonym for the words in **bold**. Check your answers in a dictionary if necessary.

1. As long as there has been crime, there have been ways to **solve it**.
a. find and catch the criminals
b. prevent and record crime
c. prosecute and punish crime

2. One of the oldest methods is **interrogation**.
a. interview
b. discussion
c. questioning

3. This system allows people to give information to the police **anonymously**.
a. in person
b. without giving their names
c. using the telephone

4. In some cases, **law enforcement personnel** have difficulty finding a criminal.
a. members of the public
b. witnesses
c. members of the police

5. Each person's fingerprint is **unique**.
a. individual
b. similar
c. recognizable

6. There were some cases where **nannies** were accused of abusing the children they were paid to take care of.
a. friends
b. relatives
c. babysitters

7. Each person, with the exception of **identical siblings**, has a unique DNA coding system.
a. brothers and sisters
b. relatives
c. twins

2 Using your notes to answer test questions

One reason for taking notes is so that you can remember what you have heard well enough to answer questions on a test or quiz. Sometimes in college classes, the professor will provide questions before you hear a lecture. Thinking about these questions ahead of time will help you focus on the main ideas and important details as you listen to the lecture and take notes.

A Read these questions before you listen to the second part of the lecture. Make sure you understand what the questions mean.

1. Professor Anglin talks about interrogation as an important part of solving crimes. What is interrogation and how is it helpful?

2. A "crime hotline" is a system that the police sometimes use to find criminals. It involves asking private citizens to give information to the police. Private citizens make an anonymous phone call or log onto a Web site anonymously. Who is likely to use this system, and why?

3. Using fingerprints is one of the oldest ways of identifying a criminal. Why are fingerprints one of the most useful tools in crime investigations?

4. Psychological profiling is a crime-solving technique practiced by criminal psychologists. What does psychological profiling involve?

5. Hidden cameras make it possible to record all activity in the area covered by the camera. What is controversial about this form of crime detection?

6. The analysis of DNA found at the scene of a crime is a relatively new and effective technique for solving crimes. Is it always accurate?

B Watch or listen to Part 2 of the lecture and take notes on your own paper using an organizational format of your choice. Listen carefully for the answers to the questions above.

C Clarify your notes if necessary. Then work with a partner and take turns giving oral answers to the questions in Step A. Do not look at your notes while you are speaking.

1 Applying what you have learned  N S

A Look in newspapers and magazines for an article about a crime investigation or a trial. Make notes about the following questions.

 1. What happened?

 2. Who was involved?

 3. Where did it take place?

 4. When did it take place?

B Review the various methods for solving crimes that Professor Anglin explained. Were any of these methods mentioned in the crime investigation or trial that you read about?

 • crime hotlines

 • interrogation

 • fingerprinting

 • psychological profiling

 • hidden cameras

 • DNA evidence

C Tell a partner about the article you read and the crime-solving methods the article mentioned.

2 Thinking critically about the topic S

Work in a small group. Look at the cartoon and discuss the following questions.

"KICKBACKS, EMBEZZLEMENT, PRICE FIXING, BRIBERY... THIS IS AN EXTREMELY. HIGH-CRIME AREA."

 1. What do you think the terms *kickbacks* and *price fixing* might refer to?

 2. Can you describe some white-collar crimes that happened in the past? Do you know about any that have happened recently?

 3. Do you believe that white-collar crime is punished severely enough? Explain.

Chapter 8
Controlling Crime

Look at the photograph of a prison yard and answer the questions with a partner.

1. What emotions does this photograph provoke in you?

2. What do you know about prisons in the United States?

1 Getting Started

In this section, you are going to discuss the problem of how to control crime. Then you will listen to people express opinions about various crimes, decide how certain the people are of their opinions, and discuss whether or not you agree with them.

1 Reading and thinking about the topic V S

A Read the following passage.

Violent crime has dropped in the United States in recent years, but the overall crime rate is still alarmingly high. Crime control is one of the most difficult and controversial subjects in sociology. People have very different beliefs about the best way to lower the crime rate.

Many people believe that "prevention is better than cure," meaning that the best way to control crime is *deterrence* – to stop crime from happening in the first place. This might mean developing educational and social programs to discourage young people from becoming involved in criminal activity, or having more police officers on the streets. Other people think that the best way to control crimes is to have tougher punishments. This might include having stricter laws, more arrests, and longer prison terms.

B Answer the questions according to the information in the passage.

1. What are two different approaches to controlling crime?
2. How could educational and social programs help lower the crime rate?

C Read these questions and share your answers with a partner.

1. Which of the two different approaches to controlling crime do you think is more effective? Why?
2. Do you think your community has a high crime rate or a low crime rate? Explain.

2 Examining graphics Ⓢ

A Look at the illustration below. It shows how often, on average, crimes are committed in the United States. Fill in the blank with the crime you think is represented by each clock. Then compare your answers with a partner.

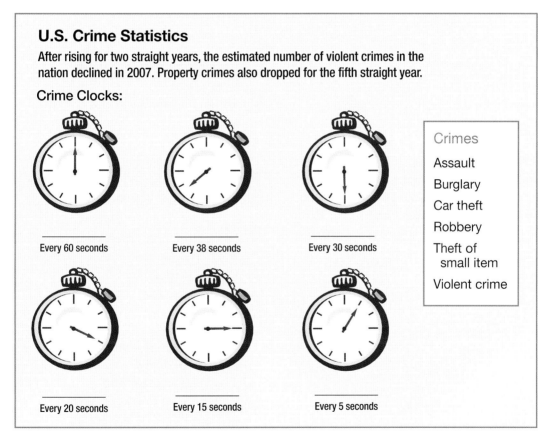

U.S. Crime Statistics

After rising for two straight years, the estimated number of violent crimes in the nation declined in 2007. Property crimes also dropped for the fifth straight year.

Crime Clocks:

Every 60 seconds

Every 38 seconds

Every 30 seconds

Every 20 seconds

Every 15 seconds

Every 5 seconds

Crimes

Assault

Burglary

Car theft

Robbery

Theft of small item

Violent crime

Source: U.S. Department of Justice/Federal Bureau of Investigation

B Check your answers at the bottom of the page. Did any of the information surprise you?

Theft of small item: every 5 seconds
Burglary: Every 15 seconds
Violent crime: Every 20 seconds
Car theft: Every 30 seconds
Assault: Every 38 seconds
Robbery: every 60 seconds
Answers:

C Look at this graph and answer the questions with a partner.

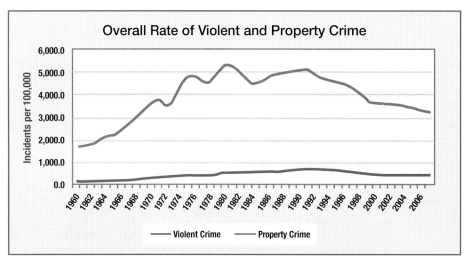

Source: U.S. Department of Justice, Bureau of Justice Statistics

1. What does the graph show about crime in the United States between 1960 and 2006?
2. What doesn't the graph show? What other information would you like to know?

3 Listening for opinions 🅛 🅢 🆅

When people are discussing ideas, particularly if the ideas are complex or controversial, you often have to listen closely to understand their opinions. You can hear how strongly a person feels about a topic by listening to the speaker's words and their degree of certainty. Look at the following examples.

The speaker gives an opinion.	*I think . . .* *I believe . . .* *I feel that . . .* *In my opinion. . .*
The speaker is very sure of his or her opinion.	*I really think . . .* *I really believe . . .* *I am convinced that . . .* *I am certain that . . .* *That's an excellent idea!* *That's terrible!* *That's awful!*
The speaker is not really sure of his or her opinion.	*Mmm . . . well . . . let me see . . .* *Well . . . maybe . . .* *I don't know . . .* *I guess . . .* *I'm not really sure, but . . .*

A Read the technical terms and definitions for various types of crime and the examples.

Type of crime	Example
1. Assault and robbery: Attacking someone and stealing their possessions	A group of teenagers between the ages of 15 and 17 attack an old man as he walks home. They steal his wallet and beat him with a baseball bat, leaving him unconscious on the sidewalk.
2. Abduction: Taking a person against his or her will	A woman who is divorced from her husband secretly takes the couple's 13-year-old son and runs off with him to another country. The father and mother share custody of the son.
3. Vandalism: Destroying property	Some teenagers break into a school cafeteria and smash all the plates. Then they spray-paint the walls.
4. Delinquent payment: Not paying money that you owe	A couple who are renting an apartment have not paid their rent for the last three months.
5. Impersonation / Breaking and entering: Pretending to be someone else and entering somewhere illegally	A man knocks on the door of an elderly woman's house, pretending to be a TV repairman. Once inside, he asks to use the bathroom, but, instead, he goes into the bedroom and steals money and jewelry.
6. False ID: Having identification papers that identify you as someone else	An 18-year-old makes a copy of his friend's college ID. He uses it to pretend he is 21.

B Listen to people express their opinions about the crimes in Step A. Listen carefully to what they say and the degree of certainty with which they express their opinions. Circle the degree of certainty that the speaker expresses.

1. Sure   Not sure
2. Sure   Not sure
3. Sure   Not sure
4. Sure   Not sure
5. Sure   Not sure
6. Sure   Not sure

C Compare your answers with a partner. Tell your partner about any of the cases where you disagree with the people you heard.

2 Real-Life Voices

In this section, you will hear David, a young man who works with high school students, talk about the importance of preventing juvenile crime (crime committed by young people). Then Amy will give a lawyer's perspective on crime control.

BEFORE THE INTERVIEWS

Sharing your opinion Ⓢ Ⓝ

A Read the community brochure about ways to prevent crime. Make notes about why the suggestions are good (an example has been done for you). Then choose the three suggestions that you like the best.

PREVENTING CRIME IN YOUR NEIGHBORHOOD

1. Volunteer to work with high school students, so that they feel connected to their neighbors.

2. Improve relationships between the police and the community, so that they understand and respect one another.

3. Clean up the neighborhood and repair old buildings, so that there is a feeling of safety in the streets. This is called the "broken windows theory."

4. Repair the parks and recreation areas, so that young people have a place to go after school.

5. Encourage shops to be well lit after dark and to welcome people who need to get out of the cold, so that streets feel safe.

6. Report all crimes or suspicious activities to the police, so that they know how people feel.

7. Educate young people about the dangers of guns and drugs by making statistics available to them.

8. Write to your politicians and ask them to spend money on making neighborhoods safe.

9. Teach students and employees, at school and at work, how to control their emotions.

Example:
I think number 1 is a good idea because adolescents need positive role models so that they will not get involved in illegal activities.
I have learned that most crimes are committed by young people.

B Work in a small group and share your opinions about which suggestions you like best.

1 Examining vocabulary in context Ⓥ

Here are some words and phrases from the interview with David, printed in **bold** and given in the context in which you will hear them. They are followed by definitions.

I think the media **exacerbates** the problem: *makes worse*

We have thousands of security guards in the schools and **metal detectors**, too: *machines that can detect guns, knives, and other weapons made of metal . . . and the kids get* **searched** *as they go into school: physically examined*

Put them on a **one-to-one basis**, and they're usually very friendly: *with one other person*

The problem is that social support systems have really
fallen apart: *become ineffective*

Kids should be doing . . . a **structured** program of activities: *organized*

The **funding** for programs like those has been cut: *money*

But we also need **harsher** punishments: *stronger, more serious*

Drug crimes carry a maximum **sentence** of 20 years or life imprisonment: *punishment*

2 Listening for main ideas Ⓛ Ⓝ Ⓢ

A Read these questions before you listen to the interview with David.

1. What does David think causes young people to commit crimes?

_____

2. Does David believe that schools are usually bright, welcoming places?

_____

3. How do kids feel about school?

_____

4. Does David believe that some kids are violent by nature?

_____

5. What kinds of programs does David think schools should organize?

_____

6. Does David believe in harsh punishments?

_____

B Now listen to the interview. Take notes about the answers to the questions in Step A. Then write your answers in complete sentences.

C Work with a partner. Take turns telling each other your answers and share your answers as a class.

INTERVIEW 2 The Prison Experience

1 Examining vocabulary in context Ⓥ

Here are some words and phrases from the interview with Amy, printed in **bold** and given in the context in which you will hear them. They are followed by definitions.

What . . . really works – not for hardened criminals, but for **first-time offenders**?: *people who commit a crime for the first time*

The first step, of course, is **deterrence**: *stopping people from committing crime*

Criminals are not being **rehabilitated**: *taught how to have a socially acceptable way of life*

You end up having a lot of people in prisons who are not the **kingpins** of drug deals: *most important people*

We need to make prison a less **repressive** experience: *cruel and severe*

We also need **bridge programs**: *programs that help released prisoners adjust to society*

Most criminals are **recidivists**: *repeat criminals*

. . . so that society doesn't look at released prisoners in such a **disdainful** way: *disrespectful, critical*

. . . so that no **stigma** is attached: *shame*

2 Listening for main ideas 🅛 🅢

🔊 **A** Listen to the interview and fill in the chart with the main ideas that Amy discusses.

	What Amy thinks should happen	The present situation
Before a person is convicted of a crime and sent to prison	*There should be more jobs and more social support systems.*	
While a convicted criminal is in prison		
After a person is released from prison		

B Compare your completed chart with a partner.

3 Listening for contrasting ideas 🅛 🅢

If speakers are contrasting two ideas, they often emphasize two words or phrases. Look at the following example from the interview with David.

The kids don't feel like they're going to SCHOOL; they feel like they're going to JAIL.

🔊 **A** Read these questions and answers. Then listen to the excerpts from the interviews.

Excerpt 1

David is discussing violent students.
Which of the following statements best represents his opinion?
  a. Some students are violent in class but friendly on a one-to-one basis.

  b. Some students are violent when they are young, but less violent when they are older.

  c. Some students look violent, but they aren't really violent.

Excerpt 2

The interviewer asks David what should be done about kids who really do commit crimes.
Which of the following statements best represents David's opinion?
  a. Small punishments are better than harsh punishments.

  b. Prevention is better than punishment.

  c. Parents, not teachers, are responsible.

Excerpt 3

Amy is talking about how to control crime.
Which of the following statements best represents Amy's opinion?
  a. It's better to stop crime from happening than to punish it.

  b. It's better to provide rehabilitation programs inside prison, rather than wait for the criminal to come out of prison.

  c. It's better to provide education than psychological help.

Excerpt 4

Amy is talking about the prison population.
Which of the following statements best represents Amy's opinion?

    a. Prisons punish younger people more than older people.

    b. Prisons punish the "small fish" more than the "big fish."

    c. Some states punish crimes more harshly than other states.

B Work with a partner. Circle the best answer for each excerpt you heard. Check your answers with another pair. What words did the speakers emphasize?

AFTER THE INTERVIEWS

1 Applying what you have heard ⓢ

A Experts have established various reasons why the overall crime rate has dropped in recent years. Read their reasons.

Reasons why crime has dropped

    1. The police are working more effectively. They are using cameras on the streets, and there are metal detectors in the schools.

    2. There are better programs to keep young people involved in sports and educational programs.

    3. The percentage of young people is lower than it was in the past. The average age is now over 35. Most crimes are committed by young people.

    4. There is more support for unemployed people than there was in the past.

    5. There is high unemployment now, so more people stay at home and this makes neighborhoods safer.

B Work in a small group. Which reasons do you think David and Amy would agree with? Which would they disagree with? What reasons might they add?

> *Ex. Some experts say that metal detectors in schools help to reduce crime. But David disagrees. He says that metal detectors present the wrong message to kids. They don't feel like they are in school; they feel like they are in jail.*

2 Examining graphics Ⓢ

A Look at the map. It shows the incarceration rate per 100,000 people in different countries. *Incarceration* means being put into prison.

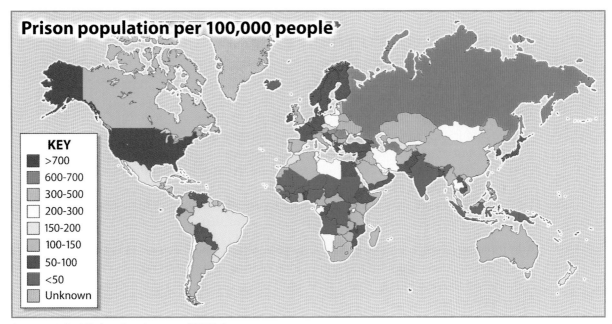

Prison population per 100,000 people

KEY
- >700
- 600-700
- 300-500
- 200-300
- 150-200
- 100-150
- 50-100
- <50
- Unknown

Source: United Nations Development (UNDP) Report

B Discuss the following questions with a partner.

1. Where is the prison population the highest? Where is it the lowest?

2. What is your reaction to the information in the map? Does any of the information surprise you? If so, why?

3. Why do you think the prison population is higher in some parts of the world than it is in others?

3 In Your Own Voice

In this section, you will examine David's and Amy's arguments, develop your own supporting ideas for your opinion about controlling crime, and share your opinion with a group.

Supporting your opinion Ⓢ Ⓝ

When you present your opinion on a controversial topic, it is important to:
Clearly state your viewpoint
Support your viewpoint with reasons and/or examples
Link your ideas with transitional words or phrases such as the ones below
* *first, first of all, first and foremost, to begin with*
* *in addition, secondly, also, then, as well as, additionally,* furthermore,* moreover**
* *finally, last but not least*
* These words are very formal and used more often in writing than in speaking

A In the interviews, both David and Amy strengthen their viewpoints with three supporting ideas. Look at the summaries of their arguments below. In each statement, underline the main idea. Then circle each piece of supporting information and highlight transitional words.

1. David believes that in order to control juvenile crime, we should try to prevent it from happening. He says that to begin with, we should have more structured after-school activities for young people. We should also have Big Brother/Big Sister programs. In addition, we need better social support systems. And, finally, we should have harsher punishments for crimes because these would act as deterrents.

2. Amy believes that there should be stronger rehabilitation programs for criminals. First of all, there should be educational programs in prison, so that prisoners learn the skills they need to succeed when they are released from prison. Furthermore, there should be psychological programs, and criminals should discuss their situation. Last but not least, there should be bridge programs to help released criminals enter productive, crime-free lives.

B What is your opinion about controlling crime? Write *Y* (yes) or *N* (no) next to the following questions.

___ **1.** Do you think deterrence (preventing crime) is more important than punishment?

___ **2.** Do you believe in having harsh punishments for breaking the law?

___ **3.** Do you think criminals deserve a second chance?

___ **4.** Do you think that some people are naturally more aggressive than others?

___ **5.** Do you think that violence on TV leads to violence in society?

___ **6.** Do you think having strong family relationships reduces crime?

___ **7.** Do you think that living in a safe neighborhood is the most important factor in choosing where to live?

___ **8.** Do you think it is possible to prevent most crimes from happening in the first place?

___ **9.** Do you believe crime is the most important issue in society today?

___**10.** Do you think that white-collar crime is more serious than blue-collar crime?

C Select one of the questions above. Write two or three reasons to support your opinion.

> Ex. *Crime is the most important issue in society.*
>
> – *Crime is really high.*
>
> – *Many people are worried about crime.*
>
> – *If we reduce crime, everyone's life will improve.*

D Explain your opinion to a small group, using transitional phrases to link your supporting information.

> Ex. *As far as I'm concerned, crime is the most important issue in society. My first reason is that crime is really high. I was surprised to learn that there is a violent crime in the United States every 20 seconds. Second, I know that many people are worried about crime. And then lastly, I think that . . .*

> Ex. *Well, in my opinion, white-collar crime is really serious. First, just look at the problems with the world economy and ask yourself: Who's responsible? Then think about the millions of people who have lost their jobs or their homes. I think it's clear . . .*

E As a class, discuss the ideas and make a master list of the supporting details you gathered for each argument.

4 Academic Listening and Note Taking

In this section, you will hear and take notes on a two-part lecture given by Jonathan Stack, a filmmaker who has made several documentaries on prisons. Mr. Stack frequently lectures on criminal justice. The title of this lecture is "The Death Penalty."

BEFORE THE LECTURE

1 Examining graphics ⓢ

A Look at the graph below. It shows the number of prisoners executed (put to death) in the United States between 1976 and the present.

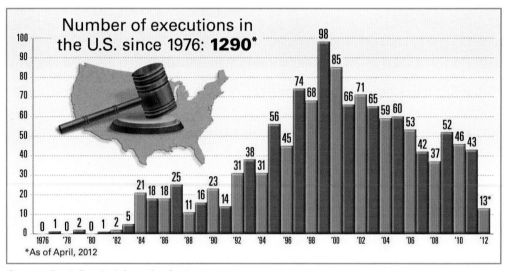

Source: Death Penalty Information Center

B Discuss these questions with a partner.

1. What does the graph show about the death penalty in the United States?

2. What is your reaction to the information in the graph?

2 Recording numerical information Ⓝ Ⓛ

Lecturers often present numerical information when they refer to research studies and other examples that support their ideas. It is important to listen to the context of the numerical information so that you understand what the numbers represent. Here are some examples of what numbers can represent.

• a year (examples: 1983, 1832)

• a percentage (examples: 20 percent, 44 percent)

• a fraction (examples: one-eighth, three-quarters)

A Read the following descriptions. Each of them refers to numerical information that you will hear in the lecture.

_____ **1.** The date the U.S. Supreme Court ruled that capital punishment was unconstitutional (*Capital punishment* is another term for the death penalty.)

_____ **2.** The date when capital punishment was reinstated

_____ **3.** The number of executions that have been carried out since capital punishment was reinstated

_____ **4.** The percentage of people in the United States who say they favor the death penalty in cases of murder

_____ **5.** The people in the United States who say they favor the death penalty in cases of murder, expressed as a fraction

_____ **6.** The number of murders per 100,000 people per year in the United States

_____ **7.** The number of murders per 100,000 people per year in Japan

_____ **8.** The number of murders per 100,000 people per year in France

B Now watch or listen to excerpts from the lecture. Write the correct numbers in the blanks in Step A. Then compare your answers with a partner.

LECTURE PART 1 Arguments Against the Death Penalty

1 Guessing vocabulary from context Ⓥ

The following items contain important vocabulary from Part 1 of the lecture. Work with a partner. Using the context and your knowledge of related words, circle the letter of the best synonym for the words in **bold**. Check your answers in a dictionary if necessary.

1. The U.S. Supreme Court ruled that capital punishment was **unconstitutional**.
   a. illegal   b. immoral   c. impossible

2. But later, the Court **reinstated** it.
   a. continued to discuss it   b. put it back in place   c. repeated its argument

3. Executions are usually carried out by **lethal** injection or electrocution.
   a. cruel   b. deadly   c. painless

4. States with the most executions are also the states with the highest **homicide** rates.
   a. assault   b. fraud   c. murder

5. I have another major **objection to** capital punishment.
   a. interest in   b. criticism of   c. opinion about

6. They were released because they were **improperly** convicted.
   a. immediately   b. angrily   c. incorrectly

7. There were 26 people **on death row**, and 13 of them were released.
   a. waiting to go to court   b. freed   c. waiting for execution

8. That should not be in the **domain** of the state.
   a. interest   b. world   c. power

2 Using your notes to ask questions and make comments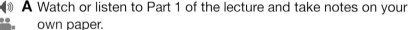

Many professors in English-speaking countries expect you to ask questions and make comments during or after their lectures. In this way, you can ask lecturers to clarify information and add your own opinion to the discussion. This makes the lecture more interesting for everybody.

In Chapter 7, you practiced writing questions in the margins to remind yourself to clarify information that you did not understand. You can also use the margins to write comments that you would like to make. Here are some reasons you might want to ask a question or make a comment.

- You did not understand something the speaker said and want clarification.
- You would like additional information about some point of the lecture.
- You want to contribute additional information about a point of the lecture.
- You disagree with something the speaker said and want to discuss it.
- You agree with something the speaker said and want to express your support.

Even if you do not have a question or comment, it is a good idea to take notes on questions and comments of other students. You should also take notes on the lecturer's response and any class discussion that follows. This will increase your knowledge and understanding of the topic.

A Watch or listen to Part 1 of the lecture and take notes on your own paper.

B Write your questions and comments in the margins of your paper. Write at least one question and one comment.

C Discuss your questions and comments with a partner.

LECTURE PART 2 Questions, Answers, and Comments

1 Guessing vocabulary from context

A Work with a partner and read the following conversation. It contains important vocabulary from Part 2 of the lecture. Using the context and your knowledge of related words, take turns trying to guess the meanings of the words in **bold**.

Vincent: Reading about the death penalty (1) **puts me in a terrible mood**. It's so depressing.

Denise: Why? I know that the death penalty is (2) **flawed**, but societies have been practicing it since the beginning of history.

Vincent: That's true. I read that in nineteenth-century England, you could be killed even for the most (3) **arbitrary** crime. You could be put to death just for stealing your neighbor's animal!

Denise: That punishment sounds too harsh. I agree with the death penalty, but I think it should only be used as (4) **retribution** for extreme crimes, like killing.

Vincent: I think you should be punished for (5) **horrific** crimes, too, but I would still never (6) **stand for** the death penalty!

Denise: I understand why this issue makes you so upset. It makes me upset, too. But in real life, if someone were to harm my loved ones, I would be really angry. I would want (7) **revenge**.

Vincent: Well, statistics and (8) **figures** show that many people in the United States agree with you. I read that 60–70 percent of Americans favor the death penalty.

B Match the vocabulary terms from Step A with their definitions. Write the word(s) on the line. Check your answers in a dictionary if necessary.

a. hurting the person who hurt you _____

b. terrible _____

c. numbers _____

d. not perfect _____

e. random _____

f. punishment _____

g. accept, allow _____

h. makes me feel bad _____

2 Using your notes to ask questions and make comments Ⓝ Ⓛ Ⓢ

A Watch or listen to Part 2 of the lecture. You will hear four students address Mr. Stack. Take notes on their questions and comments and on Mr. Stack's responses.

B Compare your notes with your partner from Part 1 of the lecture. Were the questions and comments the students addressed to Mr. Stack similar to or different from yours?

AFTER THE LECTURE

1 Summarizing what you have heard Ⓝ Ⓢ

Remember that a summary should explain the main points of a lecture in your own words.

A Using your notes, complete the following summary of the lecture. You will need to use more than one word in most of the blanks.

The Death Penalty: Mr. Jonathan Stack

Mr. Stack said that the death penalty is the most _____ issue in criminal

justice. He does not believe in capital punishment. His first argument was that capital

punishment does not _____ crime. Some states that practice this form of

punishment also have high rates of _____ . Secondly, he argued that capital

punishment is not fair. The majority of people sentenced to death are _____ .

Furthermore, a higher percentage of _____ are likely to be executed than whites. Finally, he pointed out that because we are human, we sometimes _____ . He gave an example from the state of Illinois, where _____ . He concluded by arguing that killing someone is _____ .

Four students responded to Stack. One of them pointed out that most Americans favor the death penalty in cases of murder. Stack explained that in his view, that opinion reflected _____ . Another student said that if people committed bad crimes, they deserved _____ . Stack responded that the desire for revenge was a natural emotion, but that laws were designed to _____ . He also said that if the death penalty were applied equally to all criminals, there would be about _____ a year, and that would be absurd.

B Compare your summary with a partner. Remember that the ideas should be similar, but the words you use do not have to be exactly the same.

2 Thinking critically about the topic ⓢ

Work in a small group. Look at the graph below and answer the questions.

1. According to the police chiefs, what is the most effective way to reduce violent crime? What is the least effective?

2. Do you agree with the police chiefs? Why or why not?

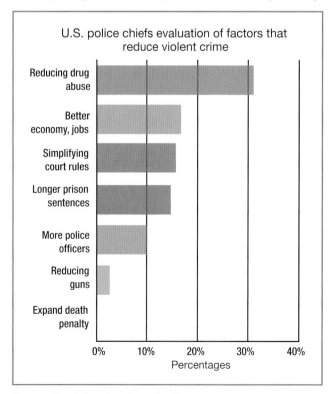

Source: Death Penalty Information Center

Unit 4 Academic Vocabulary Review

This section reviews the topics and vocabulary from Chapters 7 and 8. For a complete list of all the Academic Word List words in this book, see the Appendix on pages 181–182.

A Match a word from the left column with its definition on the right. Write the letter.

___ **1.** accurate	**a.** try to discover the truth about a crime
___ **2.** commit	**b.** get rid of
___ **3.** demonstrate	**c.** not permitted by law
___ **4.** detective	**d.** establish who someone is
___ **5.** eliminate	**e.** a type of police officer
___ **6.** identify	**f.** show
___ **7.** illegal	**g.** carry out (a crime)
___ **8.** investigate	**h.** correct, exact
___ **9.** motive	**i.** safety
___ **10.** occur	**j.** numerical data
___ **11.** positive	**k.** not negative
___ **12.** random	**l.** reason for committing a crime
___ **13.** research	**m.** happen
___ **14.** security	**n.** study, investigate
___ **15.** statistics	**o.** without a method or reason

B Use a form of the words below to complete the news reports.

> **commit (v)**   **demonstrate (v)**   **investigate (v)**

1. Yesterday there was an anonymous call to the police station. A woman said that she had seen a stranger breaking into an empty house nearby. The police _____ the case and were able to _____ that she was right. The stranger was accused of _____ a serious crime: breaking and entering.

> **accurate (adj)**   **occur (v)**   **random (adj)**   **security (n)**

2. Experts say that crime is going down, but are their numbers _____ ? Most people are still very concerned about public _____ . Crime is scary because it can be so _____ , happening at any time, anywhere. When a crime does _____ , the news often focuses on the public's fear, and maybe this exacerbates the problem.

> **eliminate (v)**   **identify (v)**   **positive (adj)**   **statistics (n)**

3. According to official _____ , people are occasionally accused of crimes that they did not commit. Mistakes can happen, for example, if a person is wrongly _____ by a witness or even by fingerprints. That is why some people think that DNA testing is a _____ step toward preventing mistakes. It is a better method of proving that a person is guilty of a crime because it can _____ these mistakes.

detective (c)	illegal (adj)	motive (n)	research (n)

4. A new novel about crime and punishment has become a best-seller. It is about a _____ who catches an older man involved in some _____ activities at his workplace. Although at first the case is hard to solve, the detective makes a breakthrough when he studies the man's _____ , and finds that he is in love with his boss, a former girlfriend. His _____ and the surprising facts he discovers, make the story really exciting.

C Use the academic vocabulary from A above to answer the following questions, in pairs or as a class.

Types of crime

1. What are some ways to categorize crime?
2. What are some examples of crime?
3. How do crime victims sometimes feel?

Finding and punishing crime

4. What are some common ways that are used to find crime?
5. What are some examples of each method?
6. Why is crime so difficult to eliminate?

Methods of preventing and punishing crime

7. What are some reasons that crime occurs?
8. What are some ideas about preventing crime?
9. What are some problems with prisons?

The death penalty

10. What have you learned about the death penalty?
11. What are some arguments in favor of the death penalty?
12. Why are some people against the death penalty?

Oral Presentation

In academic courses, you will sometimes be called on to give oral presentations to the entire class about a topic you have researched. Here are some guidelines to keep in mind.

BEFORE THE PRESENTATION

1 Choose a topic

1. Look at the mind map below. It shows a number of categories related to crime and criminals. Work with a small group, review the categories, and add as many items as you can to the list of topics.

2. Decide which general category interests you most, and then which topic you would like to focus on in your presentation. Try to choose different topics from other people in the class.

Well-known people who have been assassinated John Lennon Benazir Bhutto Martin Luther King, Jr. Other _____	Famous robberies The Brinks MAT robbery The great train robbery The Schiphol Airport robbery Other _____	Famous crime writers P. D. James Agatha Christie Robert Hans van Gulik Other _____
Famous detectives in fiction Sherlock Holmes Miss Marple Chen Cao (Inspector Chen) Other _____		Famous criminals Al Capone Guy Fawkes Jack Kevorkian Other _____
Criminals in popular culture Blackbeard Bonnie and Clyde Chucho el Roto Other _____	CRIME	Popular crime films *The Godfather* *Ocean's Eleven* *Pirates of the Caribbean* Other _____
Corporate crime Fraud Forgery Identity theft Other _____	Crimes that capture the public's imagination Crimes of passion Unsolved crimes Other _____	Other crime topics of interest to your group _____ _____ _____

2 Organize your presentation

A Organize your presentation in an interesting way using question words to generate ideas.

Ex. Robin Hood	Who was he?	A famous criminal in England. There is a statue of Robin Hood in Nottingham, England.
	What did he do?	He stole from the rich and gave to the poor. The police could never catch him . . .
	When did he live?	Nobody is sure, but it was probably the thirteenth or fourteenth century . . .
	Why is he famous?	He is very colorful and there are many traditional songs about him. He was strong and brave. He worked with a team of "Merry Men," and they always wore green . . .

B Practice what you are going to say in front of a mirror.

C If you wish, plan to take a visual aid or other interesting item to class. For example, you could find a Robin Hood song online and play it for the class.

D Make sure your presentation does not exceed the time limit your teacher gives.

DURING THE PRESENTATION

Remember that you will be presenting unfamiliar information. Focus on the most important facts, using the board to note names or difficult vocabulary. Keep your audience's attention with visuals and by explaining why you find this topic interesting.

AFTER THE PRESENTATION

Respond to others' presentations with questions and comments

A successful presentation involves not just the speaker, but also the audience. Listen to your classmates' presentations carefully and respectfully. Take notes on what they say, using the skills you learned in this unit. Then ask the presenters questions or make a comment. Here are some expressions you can use.

I'd like to ask you a question about your presentation . . .
I didn't understand something you said . . .
I'd like to ask you to explain . . .
Can you give me more details about . . . ?
I have a comment about what you said . . .

Lectures: Video Script

Unit 1: Belonging to a Group
Chapter 1: Marriage, Family, and the Home

Lecture:
"Family Lessons"

Before the Lecture
Main ideas and supporting details, page 15

1. First, then, let's discuss rewards. A reward can be defined as a positive reinforcement for good behavior.

2. Punishments are the second important way in which a child is socialized. All of us have probably been punished in our lives. For example, maybe our parents stopped us from going out with friends because we did something we were not supposed to do.

3. Parents can set a good example by showing children the kind of behavior they expect. Let me give you a personal example. I know a boy called Peter who told me he liked to study because his mother studied with him.

4. There's an old saying in English: "Don't do as I do; do as I tell you." If you say that to a child, it means that the child should not copy what you do, but instead, just do what you are telling the child to do. But this advice doesn't work most of the time. Some studies have suggested that if you smoke yourself, it's probably ineffective to tell a child not to smoke.

5. So understandably, parents are often worried about the negative lessons that children can learn – for example, from other children, or from TV. TV can send children a lot of negative messages. In fact, it's been estimated that on average, 80 percent of programs contain violent behavior.

Lecture Part 1:
"Rewards and Punishments"

Organizing your notes in columns, page 17

Hi. Welcome. Today we're going to be talking about how children learn social behaviors, especially how they learn lessons from the family – the most basic unit of our social structure.

There's a lot of discussion these days about how families are changing and whether nontraditional families have a good or bad effect on children. But it's important to remember that the type of family a child comes from is not nearly as important as the kind of love and support that exist in the home.

I'd like to focus on three of the ways that children acquire their behaviors: through rewards, punishments, and finally, modeling. First, then, let's discuss rewards.

A reward can be defined as a positive reinforcement for good behavior. An example of a reward is when a parent says, "If you eat your vegetables, you can have ice cream for dessert." Or a parent might say, "Finish your homework first. Then you can watch TV." Most parents use rewards unconsciously because they want their children to behave well. For example, a parent might give a gift to a child because the child behaved well. Or parents might give a child money for doing what the parents asked.

The opposite of a reward is a punishment. Punishments are the second important way in which a child is socialized. All of us have probably been punished in our lives. For example, maybe our parents stopped us from going out with friends because we did something we were not supposed to do. Or maybe they wouldn't let us watch TV because we got a bad grade on a test.

Both rewards and punishments are controversial. Many people think they are not effective or necessary, especially when used often. Let's take this situation: A young boy has been asked to take out the garbage. Listen to Situation A: The parent says, "If you take out the garbage for me, I'll give you a cookie." Some people argue that this reward is unnecessary because it's like a bribe. They argue that the child should be taught that it's his duty to help with the household chores, and that he should not get a special reward for doing something that's his responsibility.

Situation B would go something like this: "Justin, please take out the trash now." And Justin says, "OK, Dad."

Not surprisingly, punishment is extremely controversial, especially when the punishment is physical. Some of us grew up expecting to be spanked if we misbehaved. For example, our parents may have hit us on the hand if we talked back to them. But I don't agree that spanking can teach children anything, and sadly, some children are subject to really serious physical abuse. According to a study I just read, one in 22 children is a victim of physical abuse. Children who come from homes where violence is used to solve problems are much more likely to abuse their own children when they become adults and have their own families.

Lecture Part 2:
"Modeling"
Organizing your notes in columns, page 19

The third way that children are taught how to act is through modeling. Modeling means that they learn to behave by following an example. Modeling is probably the most powerful way that children learn social skills. Children look for role models in their life, meaning people who they admire, and want to copy.

Children's first role models are their parents. Parents can teach children by modeling appropriate behavior, as various researchers have noted. Parents can set a good example by showing children the kind of behavior they expect. Let me give you a personal example. I know a boy called Peter who told me he liked to study because his mother studied with him. This is an important lesson that he learned just by copying his mother's behavior.

There's an old saying in English: "Don't do as I do; do as I tell you." If you say that to a child, it means that the child should not copy what you do, but instead, just do what you are telling the child to do. But this advice doesn't work most of the time. Some studies have suggested that if you smoke yourself, it's probably ineffective to tell a child not to smoke.

The child will most likely think, "Well, my mother smokes, so why shouldn't I?"

Modeling is the most important way that children learn. And of course, parents are not the only people teaching children. Other family members and friends are also models. Many people do not even realize the impact they can have on a child that they know, but children carefully watch other people around them, and notice the way they behave. It's important to note here that it is common for babysitters, relatives, and child-care centers to take care of children, as well as parents. So children are exposed to many models of behavior. They learn from each other, from their teachers, and from society itself. So understandably, parents are often worried about the negative lessons that children can learn – for example, from other children, or from TV. TV can send children a lot of negative messages. In fact, it's been estimated that, on average, 80 percent of programs contain violent behavior.

I'd like to conclude by reminding you, again, that the most important thing for children is to grow up in an environment where there are fair rules that are clearly established and followed consistently by everyone. If the child knows what the expectations are, he or she will find it much easier to acquire "good behavior."

And if the child is loved and exposed to strong, positive role models, the child will quickly begin to grow in a healthy way.

Chapter 2: The Power of the Group

Lecture:
"Culture Shock: Group Pressure in Action"
Before the Lecture
Organizational phrases, page 34

The subject of today's lecture is Culture Shock: Group Pressure in Action.

I'm going to focus on three main ideas of this lecture.

First of all, we will consider the reasons why people experience culture shock.

Secondly, I will describe the different stages of the experience.

And finally, I'll mention some possible applications of this research.

First, then, why do people experience culture shock?

Now let's turn to the different stages of culture shock.

To conclude, let's look at some practical applications of the research.

Lecture Part 1:
"Reasons for Culture Shock"
Organizing your notes in outline form, page 35

The subject of today's lecture is Culture Shock: Group Pressure in Action.

Culture shock, as you know, is the term used to describe the experience many people have when they travel to another country, and it can be seen as a manifestation of group pressure in action. It is a good example of group pressure because it shows what happens when an individual suddenly, um, experiences different cultural rules – the rules of another cultural group. Now culture shock is a complex phenomenon, but [slight pause] I'm going to focus on three main ideas of this lecture. First of all, we will consider the reasons why people experience culture shock. Secondly, I will describe the different stages of the experience. And finally, I'll mention some possible applications of this research, because, although you might think that culture shock affects, say, only travelers, that is not the case. In fact, cross-cultural studies have immense practical value for modern society.

First, then, why do people experience culture shock? Think about this for a minute. When you grow up in a particular set of surroundings, naturally you get used to the rules and guidelines that govern, uh, the behavior of the people around you. In a sense, you become totally dependent on the rules of, of your social group. You tend not to question them; you just accept them without thinking. Now, these rules are often not clearly articulated, and therefore, you're not aware of their impact. In other words, you are not necessarily conscious of them. They only become, uh, important when, for example, you go to another country or a different environment

that's, uh, governed by a different set of rules. In fact, this experience can be so shocking that it has been compared to having a bucket of cold water thrown over you. Now, culture shock happens precisely because you cannot use your own culture as a map to guide your own behavior and your own understanding of what surrounds you. You're totally out of control, just as if you were driving along a highway in the dark, without a road map. And because of this, uh, people often behave irrationally. It's a highly stressful experience, and there are different symptoms in different stages.

Lecture Part 2:
"Stages of Culture Shock"
Using a lecturer's diagrams and charts, page 37

Now, let's turn to the different stages of culture shock. Um, most researchers agree that there are three main stages. If you were to depict it on paper, you might draw a "wave" shape. Uh, the first stage, the "crest" or highest part of the wave, is often referred to as the "honeymoon" stage. It's the time when you first arrive in a new, uh, culture and are confronted with a whole set of different rules. What are the emotions that you experience, uh, during this time? Even though, uh, this is a new and often strange experience, people don't usually react with fear. Surprisingly, there is often a feeling of euphoria. The most common reactions at this time are excitement, uh, fascination, and, uh, enthusiasm. Of course, you're–you're–you're you're on your guard because of the strangeness of the situation. But, at, at this stage, uh, cultural differences are likely to seem exciting rather than threatening.

The second stage has been called the "letdown." Uh, here are some feelings that people experience during the phase, uh, during this phase, uh: irritation, hostility, and confusion. They might also feel exhausted, lonely, and nervous. These feelings happen because travelers, uh, and others have to unlearn their own cultural habits, uh, and, and values as they spend more time in a new country and, and are expected to function according to the ways of that place. They, they [cough], excuse me, they may feel like, uh, lost children without protection. Uh, they probably, they probably wanna go home, uh, but if, if they can't do that, they spend a lot of time with other people from their own country, in order to get back a sense of safety.

The final stage is one of resignation. Even if visitors aren't completely comfortable, they do, they do become adjusted to the new environment. Or at least, they stop feeling that they need to defend their own culture, uh, every time they encounter a habit uh or value they don't easily recognize. They might never recapture the honeymoon period, uhhh, but they're not as depressed as they were during stage two.

To conclude, let's look at some practical applications of the research. Well, remember I mentioned, um, that it doesn't just apply to tourists on vacation, or even international students. In our world of rapid transportation and–and population mobility, many societies have, have recent uh, immigrants, sometimes in large numbers.

This becomes a general social challenge, because immigrants are going through even, even more cultural shock than tourists.

Furthermore, older residents of a country with large numbers of new immigrants can experience their own form of "internal culture shock" when they see neighborhoods or even, uh, large regions where people speak a foreign language or eat unfamiliar food or behave according to–to cultural patterns brought from their own countries. Now, because cultural differences can sometimes lead to tense relationships, um, between different ethnic groups, it is vital that people try to learn as much as possible – get some cross-cultural training if they can – about the different cultures in their own societies. Because the more we learn about our differences, the easier it is to live in a world where different cultures have to live in close contact with each other.

Unit 2: Gender in Society
Chapter 3: Gender Roles

Lecture:
"The Benefits of Single-Gender Education for Girls"
Before the Lecture
Using symbols and abbreviations, page 57

I've been asked to speak to you today about the benefits of single-sex education. Many of the arguments that I'll make apply to both boys and girls, but I'm a teacher and adviser in an all-girls' school, so I'm particularly aware of the benefits of single-sex schooling for girls. Of course, I understand that choosing the right kind of education for a child is a personal choice, and I certainly respect that choice. I also recognize that there are some strong arguments against single-sex schooling, and in favor of coeducation. So in the first part of my lecture, I'd like to discuss three drawbacks of all-girls' schools.

Lecture Part 1:
"Pros and Cons of Single-Gender Education for Girls"
Using symbols and abbreviations, page 60

I've been asked to speak to you today about the benefits of single-sex education. Many of the arguments that I'll make apply to both boys and girls, but I'm a teacher and adviser in an all-girls' school, so I'm particularly aware of the benefits of single-sex schooling for girls. Of course, I understand that choosing the right kind of education for a child is a personal choice, and I certainly respect that choice. I also recognize that there are some strong arguments against single-sex schooling, and in favor of coeducation. So in the first part of my lecture, I'd like to discuss three drawbacks of all-girls' schools.

First of all, critics of all-girls' schools argue that the separation of the sexes seems old-fashioned. They point out in the United States, single-sex education was much more popular at the beginning of the twentieth century, before the feminist movement that began in the early 1960s. These critics say that having separate schools for boys and girls goes against the aims and the goal of feminists and liberal educators, which is to provide fairness: to make sure boys and girls have the same educational opportunities and are treated in the same way.

Secondly, the critics say that single-sex schools are artificial. In single-sex schools, boys and girls are separated and can't develop the ability to interact with one another or feel comfortable in each other's company. These critics say that in single-sex schools, children never get to learn about gender differences. In coeducational settings, of course, they get to interact on a daily basis, but in single-sex schools, they not only miss out on the chance to sit in class together, but neither do they have lunch together, play sports together, or join clubs together.

In other words – and this is the third drawback - single-sex schools don't offer children a smooth transition into the real world after school, the adult world, where men and women live together. In single-sex schools, boys and girls cannot become prepared for a world in which they will compete, work, play, and live together as adults.

Now definitely, these are serious arguments against separating girls from boys in school. But there are pros and cons to any situation, and in this case, I believe that the advantages of single-sex education outweigh the disadvantages, and that's why I'm in favor of all-girls' and all-boys' schools. In the second part of the lecture, I'd like to focus on the two main reasons why I support single-sex education for girls in particular: it values girls' unique qualities and it helps girls develop self-confidence.

Lecture Part 2:
"Two Main Benefits of All-Girls' Schools"
Using your notes to make an outline, page 62

The first real benefit of all-girls' education is that it recognizes girls' unique qualities – the qualities that make them different from boys. What are these unique qualities? Well, I'm going to list a few. First of all, research has shown that the brain develops differently in boys and girls. Girls can often concentrate on higher level, abstract thinking about four years earlier than boys can, and they tend to use the areas of the brain devoted to language and emotional functioning. Furthermore, they can often work for longer periods of time. Girls enjoy collaborative learning activities, and so they work well in groups; boys tend to be more attracted to visual, hands-on learning activities. Finally, as girls mature, they're often kind and cooperative. These qualities are valued in all-girls' schools.

The second benefit of single-sex education is that girls become more self-confident without the distraction of boys. In a single-sex environment, girls enjoy being leaders. They offer help to others, and they also ask for help when they need it; for example, if they don't understand a math or science concept, they'll ask for clarification. But when girls are in the same classroom as boys, they often lose their self-esteem because they have very different learning styles than boys. Boys tend to be louder; they may jump up out of their seats and wave their arms in people's faces if they know the answer to a teacher's question. If this happens, girls typically sink back in their chairs and wait for the boys to quiet down. But if there are no boys around, girls can feel free to be themselves.

Now, it's true that recently, girls have been doing very well in school – better than boys, in many cases. Second, we have to realize that there are valid reasons for supporting coeducation, and in many cases, it comes down to personal preference. And it's also true that all-girls' schools do separate girls from the real world while they're growing up. But, in the "real," adult world, boys are the ones who set the rules of the game, and these rules don't necessarily reflect the needs or talents of girls, no matter how well they do in school. In an all-girls' school, girls can become confident enough to challenge the rules. And then, perhaps, they can change the "real" world into a place designed to help both women and men.

Chapter 4: Gender Issues Today

Lecture:
"Gender and Language"
Before the Lecture
Using telegraphic language, page 76

1. … it's a question of equality. For example, when people say mankind, it sounds as if you're only talking about men, but when you say human beings, or people, then you include both men and women.

2. Why should we use gender-neutral language? Well, first of all, it describes the world the way it really is, as I said, and secondly, it carries positive connotations, or images. If children grow up hearing the word chairman, then they internalize the idea that all leaders are men – which isn't true.

3. The title of this lecture is Gender and Language. I'm going to specifically discuss the topic of sexism in language. I'll describe what this is, and then discuss ways to avoid it.

4. It turns out that language conveys a lot of messages about gender, and a clear example is what we call "gender-specific" terms. Many terms, like mailman or policeman, are gender-specific. They all refer to men – yet, there are women who do these jobs.

Lecture Part 1:
"Gender-Specific and Gender-Neutral Language"
Using telegraphic language, page 78

Good morning. Please take notes on today's lecture. Everyone should pick up his pen – or rather, everyone should pick up her pen. Or everyone should pick up his or her pen. Or her or his pen. Wait – let me start again. Everyone should pick up their pen – is that correct? You get my point, right? In the sentence I just said about picking up your pen, I was forced to choose a pronoun, and…when I did that, I faced a difficult choice about how to address my audience. The title of this lecture is Gender and Language. I'm going to specifically discuss the topic of sexism in language. I'll describe what this is, and then discuss ways to avoid it.

First, then, is it true that language can be sexist? The answer is yes, it can. Take the example of this word: Mr. What word has the same meaning for women? Well, as any student of the English language knows, there is none. There's Mrs., which means "I'm married;" there's Miss, which means "I'm not married;" and then, since the 1970s, we've had Ms., which means "it's none of your business whether I'm married or not!" Well, not exactly, but you get my point, right? After all, men don't have to let you know their marital status. They're all called Mr.

In fact, [slight pause] it turns out that language conveys a lot of messages about gender, and a clear example is what we call "gender-specific" terms. Many terms, like mailman or policeman, are gender-specific. They all refer to men – yet, there are women who do these jobs, increasingly so, in fact. So what do we do? Well, a safe option is to use what we call "gender-neutral" terms, such as mail carrier or police officer.

Why should we use gender-neutral language? Well, first of all, it describes the world the way it really is, as I said, and secondly, it carries positive connotations, or images. If children grow up hearing the word chairman, then they internalize the idea that all leaders are men – which isn't true. Third, it's a question of equality. For example, when you say mankind, it sounds as if you're only talking about men, but when you say human beings or people, then you include both men and women.

But we need to look beyond using nonsexist vocabulary; grammar is a problem, too. Do you remember the example I gave at the beginning? "Everyone should pick up … blank … pen"? Well, I wasn't really making a joke. The fact is I have to choose a pronoun. And I don't want to give the impression that everyone in the room is male or female either. So I'm facing a dilemma. What's the solution? Well, personally, I prefer to say, "Everyone should pick up their pen." I realize this is not grammatically correct, but it does avoid sexism, and as far as I'm concerned, that's very important. Incidentally, you'll find that most university professors and writers would probably make the same choice that I do. Pick up the newspaper, or look around you on the bus or on the subway, and you'll see plural pronouns in places you might not expect.

Lecture Part 2:
"Questions and Answers"
Using telegraphic language, page 79

Lecturer: Now I'd like to organize the second part of the lecture around your questions. I can see that some of you have questions on your mind, so please go ahead and ask them.

Student: Professor Gavis, I'm sorry, but is all this concern about language really important? I mean, aren't there more serious issues facing women today?

Lecturer: You know, I understand what you're saying. And of course, there are many serious issues facing women. I mean, there are so many that I could mention: the AIDS crisis, workplace inequality, the way the mass media treats women – that is, the way they stereotype women, and so on. But I'd like to point out that in addition to these issues, the language question is also on the minds of international organizations such as the United Nations, who try very hard to avoid sexism in their publications. You see, the issue isn't just the words themselves, but the ideas behind the words. Have you ever thought about the roles that boys and girls play in children's literature? It often seems that the boys are the ones having all the fun, having adventures, and so on, while the girls just stand in the background, smiling sweetly. Women tend to be pushed to the background in society. By focusing on the language we use about women, we may be able to change their expectations.

Student: I have a question about the relationship between the way we think and the way we talk. For example, if we say chair instead of chairman, do you really think we'll start imagining more women in powerful positions?

Lecturer: Again, that's a very interesting question. And yes, it's true that we don't completely understand the relationship between language and thought. So does what we say affect what we think? The answer is probably yes. I, for one, would say that if we speak about people in certain ways, that definitely has an

influence on the way we think about them. Imagine a little girl who grows up hearing chairman, chairman, chairman. What is she going to think of when she hears this word? Well, a man, of course. But we must give young people the idea that women can also enter the professional world and be successful. Any more questions?

Student: Professor Gavis, does this controversy about how we use language exist in other languages, too?

Lecturer: Yes, it's definitely receiving more and more attention worldwide. But remember that the feminist movement, which is so active in the United States, has been a major force behind the move to avoid sexist language. It's a complicated issue, however, because the issues of gender in language change from one language to the next. For example, nouns don't have a gender in English, but there are two genders for nouns in Spanish – masculine and feminine. And German has three gender groups – some nouns are masculine, others are feminine, and then there's a third category, which isn't masculine or feminine. So each language has its own gender issues. You might want to take a look at some newspapers or magazines to see how they avoid sexism in English. Well, we have to leave it there for today. Thank you.

Unit 3: Media and Society
Chapter 5: Mass Media Today

Lecture:
"From Event to Story: Making It to the News"
Before the Lecture
Listening for signal words, page 102

1. <u>Nowadays</u>, more than ever before, we are surrounded by news.
2. <u>In fact</u>, so many new stories appear every day that it's impossible to keep up with them.
3. <u>First of all</u>, there are different kinds of journalists.
4. <u>Sometimes</u>, journalists are called reporters because they "report" the news.
5. <u>Usually</u>, unplanned events are more exciting!

6. <u>However</u>, it's important not to report too much personal information or anything that is scandalous.

Lecture Part 1:
"The Work of a Journalist"

Choosing a format for organizing your notes, page 104

Nowadays, more than ever before, we are surrounded by news. You can get the news on the Internet, on TV, on the radio, and in newspapers. In fact, so many new stories appear every day that it's impossible to keep up with them. And behind all of these stories, there's a journalist. First of all, there are different kinds of journalists, [slight pause] like entertainment journalists, sports journalists, and crime journalists, and they all work hard to deliver the news, 24 hours a day, in print and, increasingly, online.

So, how exactly do they find and write stories?

Let's look at the work of one type of journalist: a city reporter. (Sometimes, journalists are called reporters because they "report" the news.) So, a city reporter is a person assigned to find and write stories about local news. How does the reporter do her work? Well, to begin with, she should keep in contact with lots of different organizations: the local police and fire departments, the offices of local politicians, and religious and civic organizations in the neighborhood.

Once the reporter has a good relationship with these organizations, she can call them to see what's happening, or they might call her to tell her about something that's going on. There are two kinds of stories she could write about. The first is a planned event for which the reporter can anticipate many of the details. For example, a politician could be opening a new department store. The second is an unplanned event, for example, a fire or a crime. Usually, unplanned events are more exciting.

Let's look at one kind of unplanned event: a crime. Imagine that a fight breaks out between four men in a neighborhood bar and one of the men threatens another with a knife. The reporter will probably see a few lines about the crime in the police log. Once she

knows where it happened, she can go to the scene of the crime and interview people. The first person she will want to interview is a police officer, so that she can get the facts. There are four very important facts that every reader wants to know at the beginning of every story: (1) What happened? (2) When did it happen? (3) Where did it happen? and (4) Who was involved?

Once the reporter has the basic facts of the story, she can begin to interview witnesses. When you're interviewing witnesses, it's very important to get each witness's full name and some other details – perhaps the person's job or age. These details will make the story more interesting and credible. However, it's important not to report too much personal information or anything that is scandalous.

When the reporter has finished interviewing people, she'll go back to the newsroom to write the story. At that point, she might talk to her editor to decide whether she has a good story. Together, the reporter and editor must decide whether the reporter has enough facts and material to make a good story. Is it clear what happened and why?

Lecture Part 2: "Getting a Story into Print"
Choosing a format for organizing your notes, page 107

The single most important question of all is whether or not the story is accurate. If a newspaper publishes a story that isn't supported by facts, and somebody finds a mistake, then the newspaper's reputation will be damaged for a long time.

For example, if the paper publishes a story saying that Bill Jones started the fight, and later it turns out that Fred Porter started the fight, there would be a problem. First of all, the public would have been misinformed, and people might decide not to access that paper in the future. Secondly, Bill Jones could decide to sue the paper for misrepresenting his character. That's called libel, and it's something that judges take very seriously.

That's why many newspapers insist on having every controversial fact in a story supported by two different sources. If two people who don't know each other both tell the reporter that Bill Jones started the fight, then the newspaper feels it can publish the story.

But checking every fact with two different sources takes a long time, and there isn't much time in the news world. Yesterday's news isn't worth much to the public, and every newspaper wants to be the first to publish a story. A reporter who has a big story will always want to publish it as soon as possible, so it's the editor's job to check that the reporter has done her work thoroughly and that there are no uncorroborated facts.

But let's suppose that the reporter has done her job well. She's checked all the facts, and she knows that she's got interesting interviews.

Now she just has to write the story! Easy, right? Well, not always, remember how quickly most people read newspapers. A journalist must know how to organize a difficult story and present it very clearly, in language that's simple but very effective. When the story is written, it goes into the computer. Somebody checks that the story is grammatically accurate, and somebody else checks it for typing mistakes. Then a photograph or video is chosen to go with the story, and the editor-in-chief decides where to put the story – on the printed page or online.

And what makes a good story? Well, there are three main things. First of all, the story has to be new. If it happened three months ago, it isn't news. Second, it has to be unusual. There's an old saying in the newsroom: If a dog bites a man, it isn't news. But if a man bites a dog, that's news! Third, it has to be something interesting that your readers want to know about. After all, if they don't want to know about it, they won't buy your newspaper.

Chapter 6: Impact of the Media on Our Lives

Lecture: "Dangers of the Mass Media"

Before the Lecture
Organizing your notes as a map, page 119

Uh, fifteen years ago, if you heard the words mass media, you probably immediately thought of television, newspapers, magazines, and the radio. But today, if you made a list of the mass media you use, you would have to add newer technologies such as smartphones, blogs, uh, social media sites, and the Internet. In today's world, we are surrounded by technology that allows us to communicate with others. And of course, technology has brought us some wonderful things, and I personally wouldn't want to live without it. But all these new advances bring us dangers that we should be aware of.

There's a lot of violence in TV shows, and many people worry about its effect on us.

In addition to making us violent, TV can also make us passive.

Third, using the media can become very addictive.

Lecture Part 1: "Violence, Passivity, and Addiction"

Organizing your notes as a map, page 121

Uh, fifteen years ago, if you heard the words mass media, you probably immediately thought of television, newspapers, magazines, and the radio. But today, if you made a list of the mass media you use, you would have to add newer technologies such as smartphones, blogs, uh, social media sites, and the Internet. In today's world, we are surrounded by technology that allows us to communicate with others. And of course, technology has brought us some wonderful things, and I personally wouldn't want to live without it. But all these new advances bring us dangers that we should be aware of. Let's begin by discussing three of these dangers: violence, passivity, and addiction.

There's a lot of violence in TV shows, and many people worry about its effect on us. For example, almost every home in the United States has a color television, and according to a recent study, TV is on in the average household for 7 hours and 37 minutes every day. And many people are afraid that children and adolescents are especially susceptible to this violence. In 1993, for example, a–a young boy jumped out of a window after seeing a superhero do the same thing on TV while he was chasing an enemy. And what about the movie where kids set a subway booth on fire? Some teenagers saw that movie and they did the same thing. Tragically, the man working at the booth died as a result of the fire.

In addition to making us violent, TV can also make us passive. You've probably heard the term couch potato. It refers to a person who daydreams for hours in front of the TV. When we are in this passive state, we may not be able to distinguish between fantasy and reality, and we may make bad decisions about important things in our lives.

Third, using the media can become very addictive. For example, how many Internet users can say they quickly go online, and find what they need, and get off again? That's just not the case for most of us, who wander through cyberspace, clicking here and there and wasting a lotta time in the process. If you check your e-mail more than three or four times a day, you might want to ask yourself if you really need all that communication. And cell phones – which these days can also be used to go online – are highly addictive as well.

Lecture Part 2:
"Advertising and Invasion of Privacy"
Organizing your notes as a map, page 123

The fourth danger we should be concerned about is the increase in advertising. You see, the media is not only interested in providing information or entertainment, but also selling space or time to advertisers. You used to be able to enjoy a TV show, or relax and read a magazine, and there wasn't too much advertising. Now, however, it seems that

advertising is the main goal. Did you realize that the average consumer is exposed to 3,000 advertising messages a day? The content of a TV program or a magazine is just an excuse, or a wrapping, for the advertising. There's an essential marketing relationship among the media, the advertiser, and the user, and it exists whatever the media. Even print media, which is one of the least technological forms of communication, has a high percentage of ads.

On TV, of course, we're used to being bombarded by endless commercials every 8 minutes. Many of us use our remote control to zap out the advertising with the "mute" button, or simply channel surf to find someplace we can escape from the ads.

But the advertisers have found many ways to get their message across to you anyway.

They use what is called "product placement," which means that they put products right in the middle of a show. For example, uh, the hero of the show might be drinking a particular soft drink, like Coca-Cola or Dr. Pepper. Or…he might be wearing a pair of shoes with the name Nike, or Adidas. You can't escape from this form of advertising unless you just turn off your set.

The problem is not just that we are being bombarded by advertising, but that the media is invading our privacy. Advertisers are more and more interested in getting private information about individuals. Every time you use your credit card, you're giving away information about yourself. Advertisers have the ability to gather statistical data about people like you – potential consumers.

Think about this for a moment: Have you ever gotten junk mail from a company you never heard of? Wh–where did they get your address? Have you ever gotten a phone call during dinner from some company trying to sell you something? Where did they get your telephone number? Well, information about you can be compiled and sold to other companies. And advertisers can study what you buy, where you buy it, and how much of it you buy, and figure out the best way to make you buy more! On the Internet, many Web sites are working extra hard to collect information about you. You can be tracked if you make a few visits to any Web site, and the data can be used to learn more about your habits, interests, and other behavior.

We are surrounded everywhere by a message that tells us that we can be better, more successful, more popular, and altogether happier if we just have more. I believe we need to step back once in a while and ask ourselves if this message is true. Is it true? Are we what we buy? What if we couldn't buy anything, ever? Who would we be?

Unit 4: Breaking the Rules
Chapter 7: Crime and Criminals

Lecture:
"Crime and Ways of Solving Crime"
Before the lecture
Clarifying your notes, page 143

Crime can be divided into two main categories: misdemeanors and felonies. A misdemeanor is broadly defined as a crime that is punishable with more than 15 days in prison, but less than one year. A felony carries a term of imprisonment for more than one year. When a person who commits a misdemeanor or a felony is caught, that person – who is called a defendant or the accused – goes through a legal process that ends with a judge or a jury finding him either guilty or innocent. If the person is found guilty, then the judge decides what the punishment should be.

Lecture Part 1:
"Types of Crime"
Clarifying your notes, page 145

Crime can be divided into two main categories: misdemeanors and felonies. A misdemeanor is broadly defined as a crime that is punishable with more than 15 days in prison, but less than one year. A felony carries a term of imprisonment for more than one year. When a person who commits a misdemeanor or a felony is caught, that person – who is called a defendant, or the accused – goes through a legal process that ends with a judge or a jury finding

him either guilty or innocent. If the person is found guilty, then the judge decides what the punishment should be.

Let me begin by talking about types of felonies. Some of the more serious felonies include burglary, robbery, arson, kidnapping, rape, and murder. These crimes are so serious that anyone found guilty will spend some time in prison. A misdemeanor, on the other hand, could be pickpocketing, fare evasion, or something of that nature. But sometimes a crime that is a misdemeanor in one part of the country might be a felony in another part of the country.

Another way in which people may classify crime is by using the terms white-collar crime or blue-collar crime. White-collar crime refers to crime committed by salaried employees in businesses and corporations. It includes tax fraud and embezzlement, and it can involve large sums of money and affect millions of people. One of the main types of white-collar crime is corporate crime. Corporate crime is committed by people of high social status who work in corporations. Corporate crime is very difficult to prosecute for two main reasons: first, because it's difficult to prove who's responsible; and second, because the criminals are usually wealthy and powerful. An example of corporate crime that was successfully prosecuted concerns the tobacco industry in the United States. The tobacco industry was found guilty of causing the deaths of thousands of people who smoked cigarettes. As punishment, tobacco companies have had to pay millions of dollars to the victims' families.

The crimes you're more'n likely to hear about are blue-collar crimes such as burglary, car theft, pickpocketing, and so on. Perhaps we hear more about these because they happen more often. However, white-collar crime can have a greater impact on our society.

Crime has always existed in society, but today there are new kinds of crimes. One example is the use of computers to steal identities. As more people have access to computers, the more likely it is for your identity to be stolen. If this happens, criminals may open several credit card and bank accounts in your name.

And, of course, they won't pay the bill, so that means that your credit will be ruined, and that's very difficult to correct.

Lecture Part 2:
"Ways of Solving Crime"

Using your notes to answer test questions, page 146

As long as there's been crime, there have been ways to solve it.

One of the oldest methods is interrogation, a method in which the police question people who might have committed the crime or might have information about the crime. Interrogation can help the police to establish many basic facts. But modern techniques for solving crime includes more complex and scientific methods.

Let me first talk about a system often called "crime hotlines." In some cases, where law enforcement personnel have difficulty finding a criminal, they turn to private citizens for help in solving a crime. This system allows people to make a phone call or access to a Web site and give information to the police anonymously. This can often be effective when people are afraid to give information in public. Sometimes a family member may have committed the crime and another family member finally decides to call the police and give information they have.

Second. Fingerprinting. Each person's fingerprint is unique. The ancient Chinese used fingerprints to sign legal papers. What better way to identify an individual? Yet it was only in the late nineteenth century that fingerprints were first used to identify criminals. A variety of scientific techniques makes it possible for fingerprints to be "lifted" from most surfaces. Then they can be compared to the fingerprints the police have on file.

A relatively new technique that crime fighters are now using is called psychological profiling. Criminal psychologists look at the crime and the way it was committed. Based on this information, they could try to understand the personality and motivation of the person who committed the crime. Then they can focus their search on people who match that profile.

In some cases, private citizens are finding ways to solve crimes as well. With a little knowledge of electronics, anyone can put a hidden camera in a home or an office. In the 1990s, as an example, there were some cases where nannies were accused of abusing the children they were paid to care for. Hidden cameras were used to prove the nannies' guilt. However, the technique is controversial because it involves issues of privacy.

Finally, let me discuss DNA. Of the most recent crime-solving techniques used, DNA is proving very effective. Each person, with the exception of identical siblings, has a unique DNA coding system. So, if criminals leave anything that can be tested at the scene of a crime – such as blood or hair – they can be identified. DNA was used to solve a crime for the first time in England in 1987. And since that time, it has become widely used and is considered 99 percent accurate. DNA testing can also be used to prove a person is innocent. Many prisoners have been released because DNA evidence proves they did not commit the crime of which they were convicted.

Chapter 8: Controlling Crime

Lecture:
"The Death Penalty"

Before the Lecture
Recording numerical information, page 160

Lecturer: In <u>1972</u>, the U.S. Supreme Court ruled that capital punishment was unconstitutional, but the Court reinstated it in <u>1976</u>. Since then, over <u>a thousand</u> executions have been carried out.

Student: I read that according to recent statistics, <u>67 percent</u> of Americans favor the death penalty in cases of murder. That's <u>two-thirds</u> of the population!

Lecturer: In the United States, there are about <u>9</u> murders a year per one hundred thousand people. In Japan, for example, that figure is <u>0.5</u>. In France, it's <u>1.1</u>.

Lecture Part 1:
"Arguments Against the Death Penalty"
Using your notes to ask questions and make comments, page 162

Lecturer: There is probably no issue in criminal justice today more controversial than capital punishment – the death penalty. As you probably know, the United States is the only Western industrialized nation that allows capital punishment. [pause] In 1972, the U.S. Supreme Court ruled that capital punishment was unconstitutional, but the Court reinstated it in 1976. Since then, over a thousand executions have been carried out. Executions are usually carried out by lethal injection or electrocution. Today, I'd like to talk to you about some of the main arguments against this form of punishment.

Of course, the first question most people ask is: Does capital punishment deter crime? Well, although there are studies that have linked the increase in executions with a decrease in homicides, a great many social scientists argue that there is no such link. In fact, states with the most executions are also the states with the highest homicide rates. So I do not believe that it is an effective deterrence. The death penalty does not deter murder.

My second point is that capital punishment is not used fairly. Nearly all prisoners who are sentenced to death are poor males. And some states, like Louisiana and Mississippi, still use the death penalty, whereas other states, like Iowa, do not. Race is also a factor. Historically, African Americans have been more likely to be executed than whites, both in proportion to the general population and to the prison population.

I have another major objection to capital punishment, which is that because we are human, there is always the possibility that we can make mistakes. We always have to question if we have gotten the facts right. According to the Death Penalty Information Center in Washington, at least 138 prisoners were released from death row in 26 states because they were improperly convicted or because evidence of their innocence was discovered after they were sentenced to death. In the state of Illinois a few years ago, there were 26 people on death row, and 13 of them were released because new evidence proved that they were innocent. These are 13 people who would have been executed by the state. So in other words, we do make mistakes, and we have to allow for the possibility of that error.

Once you execute somebody, you've done something that should not be in the domain of the state. It's almost as if you're playing the role of God on life or death issues. I believe that killing someone is a moral decision, and that it is not a decision the state should make.

Lecture Part 2:
"Questions, Answers, and Comments"
Using your notes to ask questions and make comments, page 163

Lecturer: Now I'll take some questions.

Student 1: Yes, I have a question. Isn't it true that the public supports the death penalty? I read that according to recent statistics, 67 percent of Americans favor the death penalty in cases of murder. That's two-thirds of the population!

Lecturer: It's true that there is support for the death penalty, but it is also true that people's moods and opinions are difficult to understand through statistics. I think this figure might reflect people's concern about violent crime in general. The United States is by far the most violent industrialized nation. In the United States, there are about 9 murders a year per one hundred thousand people. In Japan, for example, that figure is 0.5 [zero point five]. In France, it's 1.1 [one point one]. So Americans are understandably concerned about violence.

Student 2: Excuse me, Mr. Stack. What did you say the figure was in the United States?

Lecturer: It's about nine murders per year, per one hundred thousand people.

Student 3: I'd like to make a comment. I mean, if someone commits a really bad crime, don't they deserve to be punished just as severely?

Lecturer: The problem with the death penalty is that on an emotional level, you can understand why people want it. If you've suffered the loss of a loved one, your immediate response is to want revenge; it's a normal, natural reaction. But I feel that the reason we have laws is that they allow us to rise above our personal, emotional response to crime. This form of retribution is not the answer. The idea of having laws in a society is that together – as a society – we are stronger than the sum of our parts.

We can rise above our personal, emotional response to crime. The legal system is supposed to make us better; it is set up so that it is better than us. Individually, we are flawed, but as a society, we are strong. And more and more states are eliminating the death penalty.

Student 4: I thought it was interesting what you said about the death penalty not being fair because it was applied to some people but not to others. Could you talk a little bit more about that?

Lecturer: Yes. In many ways, capital punishment is very arbitrary. If you really believed in the death penalty as a principle, as a punishment for a horrific crime, then every single person who has committed this crime would have to be executed. But that would mean that we would have about fifty thousand executions a year. That's absurd.

Nobody would stand for that. It would mean that the state was some kind of killing machine. The fact is that we do execute some people, but other people who have committed similar crimes are not executed. So the death penalty is not applied equally to all people.

Student 5: Mr. Stack, I'd like to thank you for your comments today. I'm opposed to the death penalty myself, and I don't think we talk enough about these issues.

Lecturer: I'm pleased to be here. Thank you.

Appendix

Academic Word List vocabulary

abstract
access
accurate
acquire
adjust
adult
affect
aid
anticipate
approach
appropriate
arbitrary
area
assigned
assistant
assume
attach
attitude
available
aware
benefit
bonding
category
challenge
channel
chapter
clarification
clarify
coding
colleague
comment
commit
communicate
communication
community
compile
complex
component
computer
concentrate
concept
conclude
conformity
consistently

constantly
consumer
contact
controversial
controversy
cooperative
corporate
corporation
couple
credit
cultural
culture
data
debate
define
definitely
depress
design
detector
devote
discriminate
discrimination
disposal
distinctly
domain
economy
editor
eliminate
emphasis
emphasize
encounter
energy
enforcement
environment
error
establish
estimate
ethnic
evidence
expose
factor
file
final
finally

focus
format
function
fund
furthermore
gender
generation
goal
grade
guideline
identical
identify
identity
illegal
image
immigrant
immigrate
impact
implication
imply
incident
incidentally
individual
individually
instance
institution
intelligent
interact
internal
internalize
invisible
involve
issue
item
job
lecture
legal
liberal
license
link
major
majority
mature
maximum

media
method
monitor
motivation
negative
network
neutral
normal
obviously
occur
option
participate
passive
percent
percentage
period
perspective
phase
phenomenon
physical
physically
plus
positive
potential
precisely
presumably
principle
process
professional
proportion
psychological
psychologist
publication
publish
random
ratio
react
reaction
region
reinforcement
relax
release
require
research

researcher	shift	structure	transition
resident	similar	style	transportation
response	site	sum	unconstitutional
restriction	source	symbolic	unique
revolution	specific	symbol	valid
role	specifically	team	violation
section	statistical	technical	visible
security	statistically	technique	visual
series	statistics	technological	whereas
sex	status	technology	
sexism	stressed	tense	
sexual	stressful	topic	

Skills Index

Credits

Text Credits

Page 99. Explanation of 5 things that make a story newsworthy adapted from *What makes a story Newsworthy?* http://www.mediacollege.com/journalism/news/newsworthy.html. Used by permission of Media College.

Page 107. Survey about the impact of the Internet on American life adapted from *What Kind of Tech User Are You?* http://pewinternet.org/Participate/What-Kind-of-Tech-User-Are-You.aspx. Used by permission of Pew Internet Research.

Illustration Credits

Page 6, 72, 89, 117, 155, 158: Rob Schuster

Page 47: Eric Olson

Page 80: ©Mick Stevens/The New Yorker Collection/www.cartoonbank.com

Page 145: ©ScienceCartoonsPlus.com

Photography Credits

1 ©Paul Burns/Photodisc/Getty Images; 3 *(clockwise from left)* ©LWA/Dann Tardif/Blend Images; ©Peter Dazeley/The Image Bank/Getty Images; ©Hill Street Studios/Blend Images; 7 ©Jose Luis Pelaez Inc/Blend Images/Getty Images; 10 ©Purestock/Getty Images; 16 ©Age Fotostock/SuperStock; 17 ©Steadman Productions; 21 ©Radius Images/Alamy; 22 *(clockwise from left)* ©Digital Vision/Thinkstock; ©Ollie Millington/Contributor/Redferns/Getty Images; ©Gari Wyn Williams/Alamy; 26 ©Ron Levine/Taxi/Getty Images; 27 ©GoGo Images Corporation/Alamy; 38 *(clockwise from top left)* ©Chris Clinton/Getty Images/Thinkstock; ©Photos 12/Alamy; ©David H. Lewis/iStockphoto; ©Cultura/Punchstock; ©AP Photo/Hermann J. Knippertz; ©iStockphoto/Thinkstock; 41 ©John Foxx/Stockbyte/Getty Images; 42 ©ColorBlind Images/Iconica/Getty Images; 43 ©Indeed/Aflo/Getty Images; 45 *(left to right)* ©Tom Gautier Photography/Fototrove/Getty Images; ©iStockphoto/Thinkstock; 53 *(bottom left to right)* ©Gen Nishino/Digital Vision/Getty Images; ©Rick Yeatts/Contributor/Getty Images; 59 ©Steadman Productions; 64 *(top left to right)* ©Digital Vision/Photodisc/Getty Images; ©Liam Norris/Cultura/Getty Images; 85 ©Radius Images/Punchstock; 87 ©Javier Larrea/Age Fotostock; 90 ©Image Source/Punchstock; 93 ©Kristina Lindberg/Taxi/Getty Images; 101 ©Steadman Productions; 106 ©A. Chederros/Getty Images; 111 ©Tim Kitchen/The Image Bank/Getty Images; 112 ©David C Tomlinson/Photographer's Choice/Getty Images; 119 ©Steadman Productions; 127 ©Caspar Benson/fStop/Alamy; 129 ©Tampa Bay Times/Edmund D. Fountain/Image Works; 131 ©Yellow Dog Productions/Getty Images; 133 ©EPA European Pressphoto Agency B.V./Alamy; 134 ©Eureka Slide/Age Fotostock; 142 ©Nivek Neslo/The Image Bank/Getty Images; 143 ©Steadman Productions; 146 ©AP Photo/Rich Pedroncelli; 151 ©JGI/Blend Images/Getty Images; 152 ©Seth Joel/Stone/Getty Images; 160 ©Steadman Productions